Under Glass

Under Glass
The Girl with a Thousand Christmas Trees

Jen Hirt

Ringtaw Books
Akron, Ohio

All new material copyright © 2010 by the University of Akron Press

All rights reserved · First Edition 2010 · Manufactured in the United States of America. · All inquiries and permission requests should be addressed to the Publisher, The University of Akron Press, Akron, Ohio 44325-1703.

14   13   12   11   10   5   4   3   2   1

The paper used in this publication meets the minimum requirements of American National Standard for Information Sciences—Permanence of Paper for Printed Library Materials, ANSI z39.48–1984. ∞

Earlier versions of these essays appeared in:
The Heartlands Today: "Under Glass"; The Ohioana Quarterly: "Under Glass" (reprinted with permission); Flyway: "Cut" and "Stronghold"; Briar Cliff Review: "Controlling the Light" and "The Grotto of the Redemption"; Touchstone: "Best Offer"; The King's English: "Ricinus Communis"; Redivider: "Laying Dynamite with the Ninth Duke of Devonshire"

All photos are courtesy of the Hirt family. The recent photos were taken by Jen Hirt; all others have unknown photographers, but were most certainly family members.

Cover design by Amanda Gilliland. Cover photo by Amy Freels. Under Glass was designed and typeset by Amy Freels. The typeface, Mrs. Eaves, was designed by Zuzana Licko for Emigre. Under Glass was printed on sixty-pound natural and bound by BookMasters of Ashland, Ohio.

This book was supported in part by the Pennsylvania Council on the Arts, a state agency funded by the Commonwealth of Pennsylvania and the National Endowment for the Arts, a federal agency.

PENNSYLVANIA
COUNCIL
ON THE
ARTS

Contents

Acknowledgements

Completion of this book was made easier by financial support. I received a 2009 fellowship from the Pennsylvania Council on the Arts; a 2004 writer-in-residence fellowship from Bernheim Arboretum; and a 2003 Walter Rumsey Marvin Grant from the Ohioana Library Association. I also thank the University of Idaho for their Grace Nixon Scholarship and my family for their generosity, which they knew I needed even when I insisted I didn't.

I also thank the seven literary journals that published earlier versions of the essays; their details are on the copyright page. Based on those publications, four essays received Pushcart nominations: "Under Glass," "Controlling the Light," "Ricinus Communis," and "Laying Dynamite with the Ninth Duke of Devonshire." "The Grotto of the Redemption" was a runner-up in the *New Letters Literary Awards*.

Various writing communities were essential in shaping these essays. At the University of Idaho, Mary Clearman Blew and Kim Barnes provided valuable feedback and insight, as did my peers in the MFA program. Peter Chilson from Washington State University and Steve Pett from Iowa State University gave great early guidance. Most recently, I thank Mary Hoffman from Harrisburg Area Community College and Robin Veder and Cathie McCormick from Penn State Harrisburg for giving essential guidance on everything from covers to content. I also thank Tina Mitchell, Modest Mouse aficionado and friend, for acting like driving on roads shaped like figure-eights was the obvious thing to do.

Seeing how this book came together has left me profoundly thankful and impressed with the staff at the University of Akron Press. Thanks to Tom Bacher, director of the University of Akron Press, for his careful edits and suggestions; to Amy Freels and Amanda Gilliland for the stunning design; and to Elizabeth Armstrong for proofreading. In addition, I thank my brother and mom for their four-hour photo hunt for original prints buried deep in a closet of albums. My dad and uncle also provided last-minute identifications of people in the photos.

Finally, many thanks to my longtime partner and source of comic relief, Paul Cockeram, who has been putting up with my greenhouse obsession since 1996. Evident in the final versions of these essays are his narrative tips and his keen eye for fairness.

❀ ❀ ❀ ❀

In the spring of 1915, Samuel and Anna Hirt purchased the Lark property at the southeast corner of Pearl and Royalton Roads. During that summer, with the help of their sons Paul and Howard, they had a greenhouse constructed and started raising flowers and vegetable plants. That greenhouse is the nucleus of the present complex and is still in use today in perfect condition.

—from the "Hirt's Greenhouse" entry in *The History of Strongsville*, written in 1968 by Howard Hirt's wife, Maude Hirt

Without a glass palace life is a burden.

—from *Glasarchitektur* by German architect Paul Scheerbart (1863–1915)

❀ ❀ ❀ ❀

Introduction
Glass Always Breaks

On my thirtieth birthday, I had the blueprint of a greenhouse tattooed on my left bicep. Young men loitering in the tattoo parlor wondered what the straight lines and strong angles of beams were all about. I explained: the blueprint was a Dutch "winter garden" designed in 1737 by Pieter de la Court van de Voort. The simple schematic showed a one-room greenhouse with a loft for retaining warmth, a glass wall oriented south, and stepped benches so the four potted citrus trees had ample sun—cutting-edge architecture, not surprising for the early years of the Enlightenment.

"Cool," said one guy, "you must be Dutch."

"No," I said. "I'm greenhouse."

The guy nodded, but he looked confused. He wandered off. I'd have to come up with a better explanation.

I'm greenhouse? I am. My ancestry, my bloodline, my memories, my identity. Hirt's Greenhouse in Ohio, to be exact. Four generations

1

of my family worked there from 1915 to 2005. In 1915, my great-grandpa Sam Hirt bought the land and built one small greenhouse. In 2005, my dad sold the land and fourteen old greenhouses for $2.5 million to developers holding blueprints for an entirely different build-ing, a CVS pharmacy. My dad wanted the money; the corporation wanted the location—in the center of town at the corner of a major intersection. My brother, next in line to run the business, hoped some of the sale money would allow him to continue the business elsewhere, and it did. Today, the latest incarnation of our family business thrives under new greenhouses.

But on the day I got tattooed, no one knew for sure what would happen to the family business. All we knew for sure was that the greenhouses would be demolished. A corporate pharmacy had no use for them.

The uncertainty spread to my immediate family. My mom was ill with multiple sclerosis, diagnosed in 1996. My dad had left her in a brutal divorce after thirty years of marriage. Their relationship, once a cornerstone of the family business, had demolished itself in 2000, and no one had bothered to clear the rubble. Because of the divorce, no one was really surprised by the sale of Hirt's Greenhouse. Saddened, yes, but surprised? No. We'd all grown jaded by then. In fact, we won-dered why it hadn't happened sooner.

I'd decided on the tattoo in February 2005, a few months before the demolition, when I knew the sale was pending. It was a bittersweet time. I was a writer fueled by the memories of a childhood spent under glass, so I hated to see the old greenhouses come down. On the other hand, the financial windfall might allow my brother and dad to sustain the family business on new land, with modern, heat-efficient green-houses designed for their burgeoning online sales. The family no longer needed huge greenhouses open to the public for holidays and planting seasons. Internet shoppers could imagine whatever greenhouse they liked. Whatever jungle, whatever season, whatever glass. Whatever.

But I couldn't haul out my Generation X *whatever*. Internet shoppers didn't need a real glass greenhouse, but I did.

My brother, on the other hand, shrugged off sentiment effort-lessly. The eve of the official sale was the eve of his twenty-eighth birth-

Demolition day, looking south toward where the main greenhouses
and offices once were. Week of June 5, 2005

day. He downed a shot of liquor at a bar, called me, and said he felt like
Cortez burning his ships—nowhere to go but forward, onward, bravely.
My tattoo healed with the salve of my brother's wild enthusiasm. How
unexpected.

So the greenhouses built over four generations were demolished in
one week in June 2005. From my apartment in Idaho, where I'd been
living since graduate school, I stared at demolition photos my dad sent
in email attachments. Jutting angles of snapped frames, wooden and
metal, crusted with white lead paint. Wires and insulation from the
offices. Slabs of concrete. Piles of glass from the ninety-year-old greenhouse, the sixty-five-year old greenhouses, and the eleven others I'd
played in as a child. Broken, dismantled, heaped. Gone. I stared at the
photos, zoomed in, zoomed out. They weren't violent, but post-violent.
I cuffed my hand over my tattoo, those dark lines of ultimate permanence. My greenhouses were gone.

My grandpa's brother, Art (left), and my grandpa, Hobart (right), circa 1940

Greenhouse history celebrates the ingenuity behind advances, like the loft and benches in my tattoo. Even more history notes their demise, because if greenhouses do anything, they fall apart. Fragile glass always breaks. It's a law and a doctrine and a prediction and an apology. For example, the fierce British winter of 1739 vanquished the greenhouse at Beddington, a famous orangery. World War I drained the workers and coal from the Great Conservatory at Chatsworth, England, and all the plants died. A smoldering cigarette leveled the Crystal Palace in 1936, and Londoners saw the spectacular pyre in the distance. Glass always breaks. Still, I expected my greenhouses to last forever. They were a constant for my first thirty years. Their absence became a blue-print I never considered.

Until I started considering that absence, that is. I've spent the greater part of my adult years writing about it, about glass and light and metaphors, about privilege and redemption, about trying to figure out what it means to be the fourth generation of something that almost ended. The result of that writing is twelve essays, each on a theme, not at all chronological, each a line in a larger blueprint, a less permanent tattoo.

Why the tattoo? So I can carry my four generations and my four immediate family members as images of four trees that are perpetually thriving in the perfect location. So forces beyond my control will stop taking away my foundations. So I can stake my own claim to a place. Mostly, I just like the idea of a tattooed blueprint, a permanent plan for the future. In the simple lines of instruction and geometry, both Pieter de la Court van de Voort and I see an expectation of a time to come. We both know that this is where the sun will slant, and here the plants will thrive.

When strangers ask about my tattoo, I explain its history and my history, but I never get to the sentence about the greenhouse being gone, that all-important merger of its history with my history. What are the right words for that loss?

These twelve essays might be the right words, a stroll through the final seven years or so of Hirt's Greenhouse. The first step: December 2000, when I realize what's going on. The final stride: December 2007 with a chance encounter on my grandparents' former land that makes me realize I do know how to let the greenhouses go. My essays are sides in a prism; the words, light refracted.

The Girl with a
Thousand Christmas Trees

My great-grandpa, an Austrian Jew who called himself Sam Hirt, was naturalized in Chickasaw County, Iowa, on March 22, 1888. He had, as far as any of his descendants can tell, the classic American dream: emigrate, start your business from nothing, hang on through tough times, have a family, and die a success. He could not have imagined that 117 years later a great-granddaughter would pay $150 to get a 268-year-old greenhouse blueprint inked on her arm in a postmodern fit of rebellion against the grand narrative.

In 1915, Sam and his wife Anna (neé Hobart) built a simple greenhouse, rectangular, maybe one hundred feet long and twenty feet high. They grew some plants, and one day posed for a portrait on their front lawn, sitting in chairs, looking toothless and doughy. No smiles. Anna wears a frumpy dress; she is overweight. Sam, bearded like Lincoln, is so thin that a Midwest thunderstorm might blow him out of his suspenders. A photo is the only way I know them.

Cue the American Dream just in time for World War I and their oldest of seven sons, Paul, shipped off as a merchant marine on the *HMS Otranto*. But the *Otranto* was ill-fated, and so was Paul Hirt. Here is October 6, 1918, and here is the heavy fog off the coast of Scotland. Here are rough seas, and here is the *Otranto* colliding with a ship called the *Kashmir*, then splitting in half, then spilling its merchant marines into the cold waters, right at the end of the war. An accident. An heir lost, no body recovered to ship home. Sam passed the greenhouse to the other sons, but as the family story goes, none were as worthy as the one lost.

My grandfather, Hobart, was one of those other sons. Even though he weathered the Great Depression working as a cab driver in Columbus, Ohio, the greenhouse was his passion. He married Onalee Baker, from nearby Columbia Station. She was the daughter of German storekeepers, and she was an intellectual, spending four years at Baldwin-Wallace College in Ohio, studying Latin and Greek. With the greenhouse, the two of them set to work every day, even holidays, always reinvesting profits.

The greenhouse pulsed as their beautiful glass heart, and they raised three kids, employed the legions of relatives descended from the brothers, and became a name in the city of Strongsville. They built more greenhouses around the original structure—two quaint greenhouses with curved glass and stone floors, then two giant workhorse greenhouses in the 1940s, plus a garden store and offices and a massive walk-in cooler for fresh cut flowers. Grandpa was one of the first retail growers in the region to light his greenhouses at night with plain old electricity. In 1943, the trade magazine *Florist Review* sent a photographer to capture the greenhouses at night, lit up like beacons against a darkness that doesn't seem to exist anymore, the light reflecting off the wet brick road.

In 1973, they gifted the entire retail business to their two sons, my dad, Alan, and my uncle, Clare. Both boys had graduated Ohio State University's horticulture program, educated and primed for the greenhouse business. If the greenhouse merely pulsed under my grandparents, it thrummed with potential in the seventies. Picture three acres of glints and reflections. Interior steel scaffolding supported frames of redwood and cypress coated with white lead paint. The frames held at least three thousand panes of glass. The place abounded with thousands of plants, depending on the season—pink cacti, Juniper bonsai, white jasmine vines, seedlings of black tomatoes from Serbia, even expensive bouquets of red and white roses, flown in from South America.

My dad had married Karen Vogely, a long-haired sociology major he'd met at a sorority dance. Mom earned her sociology degree but set it aside to keep the financial books at the greenhouse. Dad and Uncle Clare grew the plants. Grandpa bought his sons and their wives houses in the suburbs, just a five-minute drive from the greenhouse. My parents bought a shepherd mix puppy named Sadie. Mom hung up her fringed leather vest, her hippie bellbottoms; Dad put away his Army garb but kept his Bob Dylan-inspired haircut. They had me in 1975. Soon, Dad slung apathy at the suburbs, trading up for a large house in the woods of Valley City, a fifteen-minute drive from the greenhouse, farther away than any blood relative had lived from the greenhouse. His parents did not approve.

He and Mom had my brother Matt in 1977, and along with a handful of cats (a Siamese named Jack, a black stray named Hobo, and a gray tabby, found at the greenhouse one morning, named Josee), the family was complete. All through the 1980s, Matt and I played in our private jungle of drips and sunrays, fronds and petals. In springtime, we watched the workers plant thousands of trays of seedlings; dirt mixed with urgency and skill everywhere we looked. During long summers, the Ohio humidity amplified by the glass, we sat in the air-conditioned office and drew pictures on Hirt's Greenhouse stationery. Come autumn, we buried our hands in the sawdust-filled boxes of bulbs, studying the photos of promised springtime flowers, their outrageous colors and petals ten times better than Disney.

And winter? Winter came with the unbearable excitement of Christmas trees, wrapped and stacked on a flatbed truck from Michigan. Blue spruce, white pine, and firs called Douglas, Frazier, and Concolor. Every December, I was the girl with a thousand Christmas trees. My parents would bring a tree to my classroom at Liverpool Elementary, and they would donate another for the lobby, by the cafeteria. The whole

Greenhouses under construction, 1940s

school knew my parents, my mom with her long blonde hair, my dad with his thick, curly brown hair and his beard, the two of them pulling up in our silver minivan, unloading free Christmas trees for the school, the local Santas of fresh pine.

Classmates knew my parents not just from the yearly Christmas tree donation. My parents were small-town celebrities, their images on TV and their voices heard on their own gardening radio show. My dad called himself the North Coast Gardener, and he did seasonal segments on the local morning talk shows, or, at the height of his popularity, the camera crews would come to the greenhouse and shoot live for an evening news segment. Eventually, an AM station, WWWE, gave him his own radio show, with Mom as his sidekick co-host. People came to our greenhouses just to meet my parents. Fans were appreciative of my dad's instant knowledge on anything plant-related; as for my mom, they loved her long blonde hair.

As I grew up under all this glass, I convinced myself of *always*. I would always scamper down the aisles between tropical plants. I would always have my pick of white pine from which to hang my many glass ornaments. I would always remember the splash of rain on a glass roof, or the cacophony of a thunderstorm. I would always be able to say, "I'm going to the greenhouse now," just like the three generations before me. Dad would always be on TV and radio, Mom always behind the scenes or at his side, strangers always stopping them to rave about the shows.

Most importantly, the greenhouse would always be there simply because of always. In my fierce perception of reality, I claimed the space as the heiress to this kingdom. Nothing would ever change. And if it did, it would only brighten, because that's what greenhouses are for—not just controlling the light but showcasing the light.

It's difficult for me to pinpoint the downturn, the moment when nothing more perceptible than a slight wilt of leaves or a lone cloud blocking the sun changed things. It's not the moment of Mom's diagnosis, or Dad's first infidelity, nor the moment of the sale, not the dark week of demolition. Those are huge moments, colossal uprootings, ships sinking and sons lost. I don't even know if a singular moment exists, or if a chain-reaction of moments made my family resist the greenhouse as our center, our root and ground and sun. It was just a few years, but it changed everything.

It starts with what is dreadful in a greenhouse: disease. Mom was diagnosed with multiple sclerosis in 1996. The symptoms she'd brushed off for years. The temporary blindness that happened in the seventies was alleviated with steroids but never explained. When she had trouble walking in the nineties, she blamed a 1964 lawnmower accident that had mangled her right toes. An MRI showed what was up, and it wasn't muscle problems with her feet. The problem sat at the other pole, her brain and spine, where there were patches of dead nerves, hardened (sclerotic) and multiple. The spate of blindness decades ago suddenly made sense. It was the MS virus attacking her optical nerve, which doctors now realize is the classic MS onset symptom. While the optical nerve recovered, the patches of dead nerves in her brain never recovered, and there would be more patches. For the rest of her life, she would lose movement, endure chronic pain.

Next, move to a decision antithetical to a family business: divorce. As the reality of paralysis lingered in the empty spaces of daily activities

The greenhouse at night, 1943. Reprinted with permission from Florists' Review Enterprises

in the autumn of 1999, Dad took up with a younger, healthier woman. Six months later, Mom caught on, making the connection between long nights alone, unaccounted whereabouts, and new numbers on the phone bill. First they were going to work it out; then one of them filed for a legal separation. The other countered with a full-fledged divorce. My memory is so muddled, I can't even tell you who filed what, when, why. All I remember is that lawyers ponied up, eyeing the family business and knowing that my small-town, high-status parents would battle to the end over who got what.

And they did. Each refused to leave the house. Mom could no longer go up and down stairs, so Dad moved upstairs. Stalemate, standoff, battle lines drawn. Their thirty-year marriage imploded in a matter of weeks. Mom took a photo of every single item in the house and made a photo album for the lawyers. She was ready to litigate for every object. Dad, I believe, started shuffling money away from the greenhouse accounts and would litigate for every dollar.

However, for many days through the early stages of their divorce, they got in the car and drove to the greenhouse together and worked side by side in their office.

Almost eighty years of family precedent said that was the way to do things. In a family business, you might be husband and wife, but you are also owner and bookkeeper, and even if you are furious at your spouse, you still have to water the plants and pay the bills. For four generations, there had been this tacit agreement that private problems stayed outside the glass walls. There were few divorces in our family; Great-Grandpa Hirt married once before he met Anna and moved to Ohio, and some of Grandpa's brothers had married again after the loss of a first wife. Of course there were affairs and betrayals, but if the situation careened beyond resolve, my family tapped into their Midwest repression. There was a business to run. Even I knew the code. It was a strand in my DNA. A Friday night fight with my parents about curfew and with whom I was hanging out might end in slammed doors and privileges revoked, but on Saturday morning it was understood that I would be at the cash register, and Mom would be at her desk, Dad at his. We'd get along as coworkers for eight hours.

If divorces and lasting arguments were rare in our family, long-term medical issues of the caliber of multiple sclerosis were almost nonexistent. No one had encountered this—not my grandfather who smoked unfiltered cigarettes, not the uncles who drank, not my grandmother with osteoporosis. I think, as the twentieth century came to a close and our family's little life was hitting a fin de siècle of its own, precedent failed us. We had nothing else. We had no way to cope. When my grandfather heard about Mom's MS diagnosis, he reportedly said, "Is it contagious?" Insensitive, yes. Selfish, yes. Ignorant, definitely. But also spoken like a true greenhouse manager, owner emeritus, always keen to what might run rampant through his plants or his workers, be it aphid or beetle or virus.

At first, in 1999 and 2000, the greenhouse did what it always did, nurturing the generations of seedlings and flowers. But something had changed. In the past, maybe there had been a cracked pane of glass here, a leaky water pipe over there, one bum planting of flowers beyond salvaging: little things, one-at-a-time crises, handled in due course and with a larger perspective. But eventually, too many crises hit all at once. Fatigue from MS made Mom stay home more and more; Dad was distracted with his affair and the terrifying reality that he was watching his

Matt and me at Easter in the greenhouse, circa 1979

wife, his business partner, slide into paralysis; my grandparents fell ill with aneurysms and dementia. I was in Iowa for graduate school, every day distancing myself from greenhouse work as I pursued an English degree. My brother remained, the only boy in the fourth generation, by patriarchal default the inheritor of the whole thing, but he was stuck. He had dropped out of college twice, leaving a negative space in the horticulture degrees held by the two men above him in rank, his father and uncle. He fell into the safety net of the greenhouse at a time when the whole thing was falling apart. It was like the greenhouse's great glass heart, unseen but always felt, could sense a gathering loss, and it thumped erratically under all the glass that could once control light so well but was now failing in the new world of disease and divorce.

Every visit home, I could see it falling apart. At one point, so much glass had slipped from panes that shards lay like sharp leaves fallen in a brutal autumn. I gathered them, studying the water stains, the whitewash, the slick algae and moss. When had we stopped repairing, stopped tending? When had we shifted from beginnings to ends? I know that answer no more than I know what Pieter wanted to plant in his Dutch winter garden, or what my dad, as a boy, first planted in the greenhouse, or what was anybody's first symptom, first lie, or first step toward the end. I do know that a lot of old glass is gone, but somehow, I'm still the girl with a thousand Christmas trees.

Under Glass

Eighty-five years after Sam Hirt built his first greenhouse, Dad and I walked through our compound of greenhouses. It was two days after Christmas, the final week of 2000. I was visiting home from Iowa, and he wanted to show me a dying greenhouse. One of the older greenhouses, no longer needed, had gone unheated for the season, with drastic results. "It's going to have to come down," said Dad.

He was excited, and his eagerness seemed unwarranted. That morning he had bemoaned the ominous economic downturn in the greenhouse business. Strongsville was booming, open-armed to the sprawl of Cleveland's older suburbs. But the newcomers were primed for the discount chains—Wal-Mart, K-Mart, Home Depot—all of which had pitched their boxes in a ring around the greenhouse. Cheap prices on everything undercut our business. Two nearby greenhouses, Maria Gardens and Slansky's Nursery, struggled through spring and the sol-

stice, blaming the arrival of the discount stores. Slansky's summer came
to nothing. They sold to a developer of townhouses. The loss of com-
petition should have boosted Hirt's Greenhouse. It didn't. Instead of
the thousand magical Christmas trees of my youth, Dad had only ordered
and sold about six hundred. Where once our greenhouse would have
been *the* destination, it was now a quaint relic with poor parking and
pricey trees. It seemed like no new customers came; only the regulars
who had been coming to Hirt's for years and years, coming to greet the
family as much as they wanted to see the greenhouse decked out in its
incredible holiday splendor.

But now, of course, even the family was not all there.

To see this dying greenhouse, I followed Dad through the oddly
connecting hallways, back to the netherworld of older greenhouses.
With his thick, short beard and shaggy, unbrushed hair, my dad looked
like an awkward cross between a mountaineer, a hippie, and a rebel
businessman. Every day, he wore Levi's—not just any jeans, but stone-
washed Levi's—and a semi-casual, short-sleeved button-down shirt.
This combination, in varying degrees of color and newness, consti-
tuted the only clothing he owned. He hummed a tenebrous song under
his breath, pausing to ask me completely random "yes/no" questions.
Had I heard the new Bob Dylan album? Bob Dylan was his favorite.
Did I want pasta for dinner? We could go to Olive Garden. Had the
dog woken me up this morning? She'd been barking a lot at foxes in
the woods. Had I put snow tires on my car? He couldn't have me driving
between Ohio and Iowa without snow tires.

Dad unlocked a succession of doors through workrooms and potting
sheds. The greenhouse hadn't been fashioned in any logical sequence.
We had an aerial photo of the greenhouse. It made as little structural
sense from above as it did from within. Sheds and rooms and greenhouses had been added over eight decades as space and money allowed.
For example, to get to the back garage, which led to the oldest greenhouses, we stepped into a hallway that had been temporary all my life—
planks made a frame and corrugated plastic made the walls. Pallet board
made a walkway. No up-to-code hallway had ever linked the two doors,

The 1915 greenhouse

which was just another one of the many inexplicable design features of Hirt's Greenhouse, albeit a perfect metaphor for the disconnect between generations. As we headed into the garage, I suddenly thought of a question I'd never asked. Which greenhouse was the first greenhouse, the one Sam and Anna built in 1915?

"This one that's falling down," said Dad. I sensed a peculiar nostalgia in his tone, almost a note of relief.

Had I known this bit of family history? Surely. The fact seemed vital. But I didn't. I hadn't known. All these years and I'd never considered the one place that might have been the most seminal. *I never knew.*

Granted, I hadn't known the original 1915 greenhouse like I'd known the others because this greenhouse was in the wholesale section of our business. From 1915 to 1965, the retail and wholesale had been one entity, under the name Strongsville Greenhouses. In '65, Grandpa and his brothers decided to split the operation. Grandpa took singular control of the retail operations. Uncle Art and Uncle Lawrence focused on the wholesale, which stocked pottery, baskets, florists' supplies, and wreaths for all occasions. They also grew tropical plants for fancy "dish garden" arrangements, which were five or six small houseplants arranged in a gift-worthy basket, often with a miniature ceramic fawn, frog, or a little girl nestled in the center. As a child, I'd been enchanted by the dish gardens and unnerved by the uncles, who seemed ancient and dirty and incapable of speaking to children. When one of my uncles emerged from the dank backworld of the wholesale, reeking of tobacco and soil and delivering a cartload of fanciful dish gardens, I'd wait until he was gone and then I'd look carefully at each miniature garden, at each figurine, imagining that the figurine could come to life and play with me. I imagined the wholesale as some strange workshop of earthy creation, with tunnels leading to the light and life in the retail greenhouses.

How was it, then, that the wholesale had officially fallen into disrepair? Uncle Art died of cancer in 2000. He had been Grandpa's last surviving brother. His wife was also long dead of cancer, so long-dead that I don't remember her name or her appearance. With Uncle Art's passing, Hirt's Wholesale passed to his son, Cousin Paul, heir to that part of the business (and heir to the name of the original lost son). Cousin Paul had grown up with Dad and Clare. They were all just a few years apart. And just like them, Cousin Paul had majored in horticulture at OSU, then joined the military, then returned to work in the family business. Occasionally, he would call my dad and the two of them would go out for a drink, then come back home and stand outside while Cousin Paul smoked a cigarette.

Within a year of Uncle Art's death, the wholesale faltered and went bankrupt. The giant warehouse of supplies was emptied. I never knew where these items went or who moved them. The few employees were kindly let go. Dad gave Cousin Paul a job watering plants up in retail. All that remained unresolved with the closed wholesale, then, were the greenhouses.

Anchored by the 1915 greenhouse, they were vacated and left to fend for themselves over the winter. No reason to waste heat on empty greenhouses. I imagined that during autumn and the holidays, the greenhouses brooded over their empty benches, listening for footsteps, the spray of water from the hose, the nearly audible unfolding of leaves, but there was nothing familiar. There was the wind and snow, and the ice of a harsh winter, not even at its coldest. The glass of those old greenhouses waited to reflect the faces of Uncle Art, of Cousin Paul, of the few employees who hung on until the end. But Uncle Art was gone, and maybe his ghost curled against the glass, trying to see itself. The employees had long since cashed their final paychecks. And maybe Cousin Paul walked through the deserted place by himself, but he held no pots, no bags of soil, and what promise remained? So the greenhouses decided it was much too cold for their old bones. They realized Christmas had come and gone, with not one red poinsettia grown under their eaves. No customers. No profit. No family. No reason to be a greenhouse.

With the glass unheated, snow fell and stayed, compressing into ice. As Dad and I walked through the one room of the 1915 house, I saw where glass had cracked, then broken, then crashed onto the cement floor. This was the glass that Sam had purchased, maybe even installed. This glass sheltered the inaugural plants. This glass wouldn't survive to see its century. Some panes had vanished. Others cut a jagged line against the winter sky. White lead paint flaked off the wooden frames. The interior metal scaffolding was slanted, like half the roof had suddenly gotten much heavier. Rusted steam pipes, running low along the perimeter, had been dormant for only half a season, but that was too long. They couldn't be trusted anymore. Overall, it was a small greenhouse, no longer than one hundred feet, not higher than twenty feet at the peak, but in its emptiness, it was huge. As the structure collapsed, space expanded.

Only the cement floor remained in good condition. There was a center aisle with raised benches on each side, and then narrow side-aisles skirting the benches. Everyone had always called them benches, even though they were more like raised tables with shelves. Calling tables "benches" was part of our family's lexicon, just like the way we said "greenhouse" (singular) when we meant "greenhouses" (plural). If we were at home, and it was time to go to work, we'd say "Let's go to the greenhouse." Maybe it was a little homage to Sam, since all he ever knew was one greenhouse.

Aerial view of Hirt's Greenhouse, late eighties or early nineties

I rounded a bench and headed down one of these narrow aisles. The sloped roof was lower here, and I could touch it, but didn't. There was something green, dark malachite, peeking from beneath the lower bench were the cement ended and crusty dark dirt took over. It was, against all odds, a grassy weed, alive and well in a space disowned. Dad saw it too.

I had to feel it. Its leaves were slender, cool, and smooth. Tenacious, thriving in winter, in a place like this. A little unreal. But the shelf of the bench yielded insulation and shelter from the draft and snow, and somehow, the weed had rooted to water. Even in this forlorn, forgotten space, the sun shone refulgent.

I asked Dad what was going to happen to this greenhouse. He said he didn't know. It was too expensive to tear down.

"So repair it," I ventured. But the cranky steam pipes and shattered glass and unsteady frame made it too expensive to repair. Its central

The greenhouse and nursery land, looking north along State Route 42, 1935

location—it was surrounded by all the other greenhouses and buildings—made it too hard to reach by bulldozer and crane.

"It won't last another winter," said Dad. "All this glass is going to come down."

"But this was the first one," I said. "It means something. There's history here."

"But financially, it's not worth anything." The bottom line was firm.

History couldn't be romantic and realistic at the same time. And my dad was a man of convenience. He managed the greenhouse as a business first, a greenhouse second. I'd seen him throw away twenty full-grown Easter lilies the day after Easter, all perfectly healthy and gorgeous, but unsellable, and I knew he'd do the same with the Christmas trees and poinsettias. When customers brought him ailing plants, covered with insects or black-spotted leaves, he often offered a healthy plant in exchange, promising to nurture the sick one back to life and resell it later. Instead, after the customer was gone, he'd toss the sick plant in the trash, not even saving the pot.

And rarely did he fix anything. When a computer monitor inexplicably blacked out, he dropped it in the trash and drove straight to the store to buy a new one. He did this more than once, with monitors, printers, disc drives, everything. When the clutch on his car gave out for the third time, he didn't try to be a better driver, instead demanding the mechanics repair it by noon the next day. When I was twelve and was convinced that my brother stole my new Guns N' Roses CDs, claiming they were his, Dad didn't sit us down and mediate and try to figure out who was right, who was wrong. He just took me to the mall and bought me all new CDs, saying, "There, now you have your CDs back." He was dealing with the collapsing greenhouse the way he dealt with everything else, like his failed marriage and Mom's illness. He avoided the complicated questions and discarded the useless.

"Besides," Dad concluded, "these benches have asbestos in them." He laughed. He'd always taken delight in the irony of bad business decisions.

I slid my hand along the raised benches. They were rimy with faint frost. Potting soil softened the corners. They probably were made of asbestos, although I didn't know how to tell. I didn't need to: Uncle Art had died of cancer, his wife had died of cancer, and some of the wholesale employees had cancer. My fingers found warped ridges, from decades of humidity and water weight. And stains, from terra cotta pots left in one place too long. Dad walked past me to the exit in a way that suggested we were done here, but I was not. This was probably the last time I'd be in this greenhouse, this exact space, this precise space, this all-important origin, but today was the first day I knew this was *the original greenhouse.*

It didn't seem fair. I'd walked through this greenhouse before, but I *never knew.* I refused to follow Dad to the exit because I hadn't had my time here. I hadn't waited for my great-grandfather's memory to show me what he really envisioned in 1915, what he grew that first year, how he wanted his children to plant and tend and water. And where was his wife, my great-grandmother, Anna? I was saddened to know nothing about her, guilty, almost, over not imagining her in this location. Why could I only trace my past through the patriarchy? Where were my other women? Great-Grandma Anna must have been here too. And Grandma, her sisters, their daughters. Maybe even my mom, young, healthy, in her final year of college, working with her future in-laws, maybe walking back to the wholesale to pick out a basket for a floral arrangement. I could see her in tennis shoes, jeans, a silk blouse, a broad smile. Knowing that this was the first greenhouse only served to show me what else I didn't know. Wasn't there some way to save this space and structure? I felt like I was the only Hirt who never planted anything here, right here. I felt like I was the only one who wasn't waiting for the place to collapse.

My reaction was jaw-clenching anger. There was no good reason why the 1915 house had to fall. *This is my history too*, I wanted to remind Dad. *You cannot just let this greenhouse fall down. You could have taken care of it. You should have. Maybe this was all supposed to be for me. Why do you think everything has to end with you?*

I looked the entire greenhouse over one more time. Then we walked back to the world of the living, where the greenhouses were sentient with life. I sat in Mom's office chair. She was home, too tired to be at work.

"So, really, what are you going to do?" I asked.

"I'm not going to do anything," Dad said, looking at me like I'd posed an impossible question. "It's not my problem. Let the damn thing collapse. I don't care."

With all the other difficulties hounding my dad that winter, I could understand his vehement refusal to care about one more headache. The collapsing greenhouse was just the most visible problem, the only one not directly involving a family member. There was the divorce to deal with, and Grandma and Grandpa's rapidly failing health. And although he never talked about it, I knew my dad had his own complex ghosts vexing him. Mom's struggle with MS had eclipsed his health problems, his severe ulcers and high blood pressure. Before the divorce started, he had internalized his own worries so as not to distress Mom. Now he was sick. He had been sick. I could tell he was struggling with the guilt of his deception and his basic need to find some sort of happiness in a suddenly bleak life. And I could tell he had stopped minding his life's work, the delicate, powerful plants under the amazing glass.

Compounding these dramas was the hitch of money. Greenhouses often operate on extraordinary debt due to long growing seasons when nothing can be sold, but holidays and summer usually cover the costs. Not this year, however. The debt from January's and February's heating bills remained on the books, even after the holiday rush. For the first year in my lifetime, the greenhouse had not turned a profit. Dad and his brother had to entreat their parents for a loan just to settle the bills. Grandpa furiously handed them the money, not knowing what to do with his two sons who had, in his eyes, failed the family. Privately, Dad told me that he thought Grandpa held over a million dollars, not from greenhouse profits, but from stocks, bonds, and real estate. Dad thought Grandpa was too senile to understand what to do with his bankroll.

"Why don't you talk to him?" I suggested.

"He doesn't listen," said Dad. "He thinks if we all just work a little harder everything will be fine. He doesn't realize times have changed. He's sitting on a million dollars and he hasn't bought a new pair of pants in twenty years."

This was true. I was silent for a few minutes, trying to solve it all in one quick sweep of logic.

"Does Grandpa know the old greenhouse is falling down?"

"Of course not. And I'm not going to tell him."

"Why not?"

"He'll try to fix it by himself."

This was also true. Dad left to help a customer pick out a couple discounted poinsettias. (Dad kept them around through New Year's, because people bought them for the last round of holiday parties.) I moved from Mom's office chair to his office chair so I could look at the framed greenhouse photos from the 1940s. Since the photos of my grandpa and his brothers and the greenhouses in various stages of construction rarely featured my grandmother, I had always assumed she was the photographer, the documenter. In my life, however, I had never seen her take a picture. In the context of those old photos, I could only assume where she was, what she was doing, what she saw.

Before I left, Dad and I stood awkwardly outside the greenhouse, looking at twenty unsold Christmas trees, each one fallen over. They were all lovely, not a reject among them. I was surprised that two were expensive Concolor firs, with wide needles and widely spaced branches. Even at $70 a tree, the Concolors had always sold out, because they were perfect for heavy ornaments or extensive garland. A week before Christmas, Dad had discounted all the trees, even the remaining Concolors, to $9.99. He leaned over and made a half-hearted attempted to lift one of the firs. It was stuck to the asphalt because the spilled water from the tree stand had frozen. I lifted from the other side, and we righted the pine, brushing it off.

Six months later, Dad sent me a single stunning email. It stopped me faster than anything else he'd ever written or said. I had to read it twice. He had written about walking around the greenhouse late at night, wondering what it would be like to be happy again. I scrolled up through the message to see what time he sent it. Four in the morning, from the computer in the greenhouse office, alone and online at the darkest hour, in the darkest place, surrounded by his past and his present, his successes and failures, his sadness and confusion.

I was alarmed. The greenhouse is eerie by moon and star; city lights cast leafy shadows, and the steam pipes hiss and clank as if wrenching themselves from the walls. Rodents forage, and plants shiver when they shouldn't. I wondered what had transpired that evening that caused him to seek refuge in the greenhouse. There were too many possibilities now. He could have fought with Mom, or Grandpa, or his girlfriend, or his lawyers. I wondered how long he stayed, and who else he wrote to. I wondered where he went when he left.

Controlling the Light

Where would any of us go without these greenhouses? In what mental state would I reside if my parents divorced, if my mom ended up paralyzed, if I couldn't do anything to stop it, just as I was powerless to save a collapsing greenhouse? I knew I was cut from my father in a way that made me more like him than my mom. I knew it was just a matter of time, of broken glass and wayward forces, before I too would be composing existential emails at 4 AM. I didn't know where I would go.

So I continued with graduate school. In Idaho. Across time zones, rivers, mountains, to a region that had nothing to do with my family. At the University of Idaho library, I went past my past to the history of greenhouses. If I could understand how greenhouses began, maybe I could understand how mine would end, as if knowing ahead of time would make it all less devastating. If I couldn't stop the 1915 greenhouse from collapsing, at least I could get out from under it.

It starts like this: Caesar demanded fresh cucumbers.

His servants fretted. How to keep a steady supply? How to predict when a cucumber would ripen? How to have one cucumber at the ready, on call in a great Roman kitchen? No one had a clue. Enter serendipity: Imagine a Roman leaving a slat of mica (a thin translucent mineral common in the countryside) propped against a pillar, only to return days later to see vigorous sprouts stretching up into the warm angle of space below the mica. This discovery must have been momentous, third to wheels and aqueducts. Servants learned to control the light using that precursor to glass. In the end, that's the whole beginning—use translucent material to control the light. Later, we'd call it photoperiodism. What Caesar demanded, Caesar got, and all the little caesars from then on had a wild hunger for light and leaves, foliage and fruit.

Take Queen Victoria. Like Caesar, she craved cucumbers. Unlike Caesar, she could not tolerate the way the thing curved, thick and ruddy, obscene. So she insisted that her cucumbers be year-round and straight. When the first nub of fruit appeared, a servant would angle it into a tube, where it had no option but to grow straight. Cucumbers came to her plate straight as laces.

But it was the orange that really brought revolution to the greenhouse world. Citrus was magic: magic color, magic scent, magic texture, magic taste. Even, we would learn later, the magic vitamin C. Europeans raised on leeks and rabbit had never imagined anything like an orange. Only a few nobles had to enjoy one before issuing the edict for more. Greenhouses dedicated to growing citrus were called orangeries, and the first one was built in 1591 at the University of Pisa in Italy.

The game was on: *to fructify in winter*, to grow fruit out of season. The orangery had to be a masterpiece of technology. It had to face south and slope at just the right angle to catch enough light. It had to have a massive heating system. It had to tolerate water and humidity. The roof had to be high enough to accommodate full-grown citrus trees eventually, yet low enough not to waste the heat that rose like angels. The whole goal was to trick spring into summer and summer into forever, all in the months of winter. Making oranges ripen in London in January was called *forcing*, and smaller greenhouses meant to conserve heat around citrus saplings were called *forcing houses*. Ruskin called the forcing houses "vile and gluttunous." Seasons had been shut out.

Ruskin, of course, was in the minority. Taste buds and oranges won.

I have been to one orangery, at the Charlottenburg Castle near Berlin. It was December of 1996; I was a student in a study-abroad class about science and literature. I took the obligatory tour of the castle and then headed to the orangery, converted into a fancy restaurant. I sipped wine (the only thing I knew how to order). The south wall was all glass, by now more for the ambiance than the light. Tables and chairs had replaced all the orange trees, which would have been grown in giant wheeled pots made of thick wood. What was once the place where servants had grown food was now the place where servants served food. I don't recall that they served oranges.

As I sat in that lovely old place, I had a clear sense of how the human race has worked hard at tricking everything. The Charlottenburg Castle is a masterpiece of illusion. Scenes of the sky are painted on the ceiling, with celestial beings charming rooms dripping with the illusion of gold trimmings. I lost track of the number of tables and chairs with clawed feet. I mused at the gigantic Salvador Dali sculpture out front. It was part of *Persistence of Memory*, the dripping copper clock slung over a barren branch, countering the reliability of time. The old orangery stood as an ancient monument to the first sweet success of ignoring the seasons, of ignoring time.

Sometimes, at our greenhouse, my dad would order a few miniature orange trees. They would arrive heavy with tiny green globes, some with a faint tinge of the orange they would ripen into. As a child, I found them absolutely curious. The first time I saw one, I begged to know when the little oranges would ripen. I thought they were for me. I was Caesar. I was Victoria. But I was told these trees were ornamental, their fruit not like the oranges from the store. No, I could not have one.

I understood, then, that plants were sometimes status symbols, like cars or houses or jewelry. When no one was watching, I picked a miniature orange and kept it in my pocket all day. No plant was above me.

Status. In the sixteenth century, maintaining the living treasures of traders and explorers was a prime goal. The idea of using greenhouses

Art (left) and my grandpa (right) in the South House

to provide produce for the commoners was still generations away. Wealthy Europeans would gather specimens of new and exotic plants, like orchids, or palms, or cacti, and transport them back home to nurture them under glass. Greenhouses were more like living museums, or botanical gardens, meant to showcase first and cultivate second.

In the 1780s, George Washington built a greenhouse at Mount Vernon. However, he wanted more than oranges. He wanted pineapples. They were so strange, each one a platypus of fruit, a body like a pinecone, a stem like a spiny desert yucca, sweet gold flesh, and huge. Taste unrivaled. One of the first pineapples ever grown in a greenhouse was immediately given to Charles II, literally a gift of gold. Like Caesar and Charles and Victoria, Washington got his pineapples. We all got them.

He also accepted a gift from King Louis XVI of France, a shipment of exotic plants. What were they? The gift could have included brilliant orchids, their bare woody stems layered with flowers, or bromeliads from the tropics, with their cupped leaves holding water. Probably there would have been the "big five" of conservatory plants: citrus trees, jasmine vines, oleanders, pomegranates, and the delicate groundcover myrtle. All were prizes of eager explorers, and they became the gifts of kings. Someone who could successfully raise such unusual plants must have seemed like a mystic to those who struggled with common corn and beans.

Everyone wanted to grow the strangest plants. If you were a Victorian, and you had a houseplant, and it tilted sideways toward the window like all houseplants do, then you were shunned because plants in the wild did not have to tilt toward the sun. You were shunned because your illusion wasn't strong enough. If you were Victorian, and you owned a bizarre fern from some humid slit of Borneo, and you kept it alive and built your intellectual identity around it, you were admired. You might have kept the fern in a Wardian Case (a terrarium) so it wouldn't tilt toward the window. Basically, if you cold-shouldered the seasons, you could become a prominent Victorian. Much of that sentiment still exists today: Go to any retail greenhouse. Notice the exotic plants. The Victorian sentiment reigns.

When I catch a glimpse of a backyard greenhouse, the glass blurry with the humidity of breathing leaves, I have to wonder what well-tended plants live inside, what ambitions and dreams the owner has folded into warm dark soil, Victorian influence or not. I think we tend plants for only two reasons, either memory or hope. People often reminisce about plants from their childhoods, recalling the heavy lilacs framing a path, perhaps even reciting a poem fragment, *"when lilacs last in the dooryard bloomed."* They will remember vegetable gardens and wedding flowers, autumn leaves pressed between wax paper, nipping dandelion heads, enjoying the not-so-bad crunch of dirt on a fresh carrot. And they will try to conjure these plants again and again. They will plant gardens like their grandmothers did.

What do I remember? It's funny, but two of my clearest memories are of losses, not acquisitions.

When I was young, there was a giant palm bush in our living room, so big in a square pot that I could stable my best Breyer horses amongst its stems and fronds, or I could hide behind it when I didn't want to go to bed. Its top brushed the ceiling, and its light green fronds filled the corner space between the couch and the chair. To protect it from our young German shepherd's curious mouth, we were supposed to put the vacuum cleaner in front of it whenever we left. One evening, someone forgot.

And so our dog destroyed the grand old palm, that prized corner piece of the living room. She took it frond by frond, then wrenched it from the square pot, building to a grand finale of dragging the root ball across the Oriental rug. In an encore, she must have shook the root ball the way she shook her cotton chew rope. We found clumps of dirt behind the piano, on the bookcase, under the dining room table, and on the stairs. Dad was angered into silence. He took note of the destruction, took note of the vacuum in the closet, and simply cracked open a beer and sat in front of the TV. Mom and Matt and I bagged its remains. The dog, banished to the backyard, wagged her tail, unsure.

Another time, when I was in college, I remember my parents relating the sad news about the untimely demise of their Bradford pear, which, in full red autumn glory, had succumbed to an early ice storm and split down its ornamental middle. They'd planted the tree at the front corner of their property, where its crimson foliage would be a focal point against the old hedge of thorny Osage orange trees. It was also in our horse pasture, and my two bay Arabians would graze around it, a picture perfect setting straight off a scenic calendar. My parents loved the Bradford pear. They took pictures of it in all seasons, noting its growth each year. When they emailed me with the news of the ice storm, it was like they were telling me about the death of an admired community leader.

The palm. The pear. Neither could be replaced.

But I also have this memory: the tree lot at Christmas. It is 8 PM and we are closed. My parents are counting the money. The gates to the tree lot have been locked, but the Christmas lights are still on, and Dad says we can play outside. My brother and I and our palm-destroying dog have those thousand Christmas trees to ourselves. Heavy snowflakes silence all of Strongsville. The three of us are chasing each other, then ducking under trees leaning against the fence, a madcap game of tag and hide and seek. I am trying to be a wolf, trying to sneak up on my own dog, and she is hunting me, her head down in stalking mode, and when she spots me from the far end of an aisle lined with beautiful thick pines, she hurtles straight at me, her ears pinned to her head, cutting a line through the snow, and I sprint away, and my brother is pelting us with snowballs, and my dog is catching me, nipping my mittens, and I'm diving under a tree faster than a rabbit, so fast that my dog skids to a stop halfway down the path and has to circle back at a trot, but by then I've dashed through the whole forest, am hiding somewhere else, wonderfully out of breath, silent in the snow, caught up in this best of all games until my dad calls over the outdoor speaker system, the voice of a god telling us it's time to go home, get the dog, meet at the office. We blunder inside, through the dark storage of terra-cotta pots stacked to the ceiling, through the florists' workroom redolent with pine and roses, cedar and fruit baskets; we race down the long rows of perfect poinsettias all tricked into red bracts for the sake of commerce.

We only calm down and stop running with the promise of pizza, and there are Christmas specials on TV tonight, and with all the snow we might not have school tomorrow. As we drive away, the greenhouse glows in the rearview, lit top to bottom with holiday lights, glowing from the inside, the glass wet and warm against December in Ohio.

There won't be school tomorrow, and my brother and I will dress in our old jeans and warm sweaters and spend the snow day at the greenhouse, watching florists cut greenery for holiday arrangements, watching our favorite clerk, Laurie, tie red ribbons on poinsettia after poinsettia. It will be the busiest day this season, and I will love watching adults work. Someone will bring a massive crock of vegetable cheese soup for lunch, of which we take more than our share, for we have new appetites, and later Dad will give Matt and me clipboards, paper, pens, and special assignments to count certain plants. Inventory, it is called. We take our inventory seriously, thinking we work here today. We already know the names of these plants, have known them since birth, it seems: amaryllis, African violet, Old Man cactus, ficus, string-of-pearls, dracaena, philodendron, Boston fern, staghorn fern. There are so many customers that we have to keep our dog on a leash, and she heels obediently while we count plants. Everyone wants to pet her. She is a grey German shepherd, like a wolf, except her ears flop like a puppy's. I think she's beautiful and that she understands me. Mom checks our counts, pays us in quarters for the vending machine, and our dog trots at our side. I get a Pepsi; Matt, maybe a root beer. We take them to the break room, just like employees, and drink them while snacking on Ritz crackers left over from a fruit basket. We think about our last name, our greenhouses.

We get takeout pizza for a second night in a row, and Mom and Dad are so tired that they let us each open a present. Maybe I got a new Breyer horse; maybe I got a Choose-Your-Own-Adventure book. It's doesn't matter. It's a good memory. It's me in a greenhouse. It's a lifetime of Christmas.

Philosophers have thought about greenhouses, contemplating the deeper truths and meanings under glass. Walter Benjamin was the first to see greenhouses for what they were. He called them "residues of a dream world. . . . The collector dreamed he was in a world that was not only far off in distance but also in time." Not far away in sentiment was George MacKenzie, an architect, who proclaimed in an ecclesiastical shiver that the roof of a greenhouse should be parallel to the "vaulted surface of the heavens." Another greenhouse visionary, Loudon, said, "may not therefore greenhouse roofs be rendered expressive of ideas of a higher and more appropriate kind?" Yet another builder, Leopold, constructed a church that was a greenhouse, a greenhouse that was a church. These men and their gods, their glass, their grapevines! In the nineteenth century, they couldn't just make their greenhouses practical. They had to advance architectural guidelines, had to honor the gothic, nod to the Roman, accommodate the promenade. And a greenhouse, back then, was very much about showing off. Dukes held dinners in their conservatories. You had an invitation, and you had a seat at a grand table moved under glass just for this occasion, dinner in a jungle. For dessert, the grand show: the servants brought in potted citrus trees, straight out of my tattoo, all fructifying on command, and for dessert you simply reached behind you, picked an orange, and ate it. Sensational.

My grandpa's brothers, Howard and Lawrence, in the South House, 1935

I think of Sam Hirt around 1915, his life culminating in a tiny, plain greenhouse. No vaulted surface of the heavens, no residue of a dream world, no royalty honoring invitations. At the end of his day, he couldn't reach for a fresh orange. Did he want to? He didn't want to. It was all business by then.

When the Disease Process
Cannot be Compared
to Volcanic Island Chains

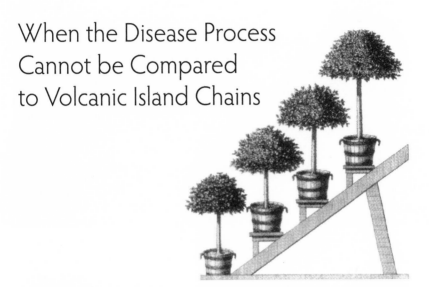

When I checked last, there were about twenty-four million family businesses in America. Hirt's Greenhouse was one of them, but certain characteristics distinguish it. For example, the family business start-up boomed after World War II. Hirt's, however, was founded in 1915. Most family businesses average two generations from founding to closure. The four greenhouse generations of the Hirt family bowed only momentarily to the Great Depression, grudge-mongering, chancy Ohio weather, even divorce and disease.

A family business can only last that long if it is resilient. But resilience asks a price. What was it? What did we tender in exchange?

My mom grew up in Pennsylvania, then Ohio, and finally Michigan, the family of four kids following the father's various engineering jobs. Her father was a man of tools and wood and talent. He had survived an eye-grazing bullet in WWII, and ever after made good use of this time, crafting furniture, houses, and even a houseboat. Her mother was a registered nurse. A spry little woman, her mom raised the kids, hosted an exchange student from Holland, and later made a hobby of owning and training pairs of black Great Danes. When my mom was in college at Ohio State, the whole family moved south to Lake Livingston, Texas. On waterfront property, mom's parents built a three-story home with an elevator, a six-car garage, a rose garden, a kit-greenhouse for orchids, a boathouse, and a two-story, three-bay dock (with three boats, of course). And there was a waterslide. They trained their black Danes to stay in the yard, no fence, their huge feet obediently stopped at the edge of the searing-hot asphalt. Mom remained in Ohio to finish her sociology degree and marry Alan, securing status at the greenhouse. She moved from one well-off family to another.

Two aspects of personality define my mom. First, she is a classic codependent—someone who insists on the well-being of a spouse and children, purposefully endangering her own well-being in the process. She did not know she was codependent until her therapist signed her up for Codependents Anonymous. She was in her fifties, kids grown, husband leaving her, disease taking hold, menopause sweeping through, and she did not know how to take care of herself because codependents define themselves through others' needs, successes, and failures. But it was the one crucial time when she absolutely needed to take care of herself.

Some examples: When my mom shopped for groceries, she stocked the cart with the ingredients for the four or five meals Dad, Matt, and I preferred. She never thought to buy food especially for herself. Her self-disinterest extended to the greenhouse. She had a natural talent for floral designing, arranging the miniature intricacies of corsages and twisting yards of thick ribbon into holiday bows. But when Grandma retired from the bookkeeping position in the early seventies and Dad asked Mom to switch to half-day shifts in the office at Grandma's old desk, she agreed, though her real interest was still in designing. Her codependency kicked in. She did it for the good of her husband, for the approval of her in-laws, for the status afforded by her last name spotlighted on the sign, the last name bannered like a headline on expensive ads run in the *Plain Dealer*. It's no mere coincidence that her first symptom of MS, blindness in one eye, now such a residual metaphor, happened at the same time.

For many years she also attended Codependents Anonymous, a self-help movement which employs a twelve-step method for getting its mostly divorced middle-aged female members to snap out of the codependent funk, to become independent, to listen to what *their* bodies and minds need first. They called the group "Coda," and they took a step a month. People could join anytime, and those further along in the twelve steps would shepherd the others through. Mom joined two Coda groups, each in different counties, neither close to her home. She was embarrassed. But soon, she was a devotee. She attended the meetings as if they were her new job.

My brother, amused by Mom's thrice-weekly obsession with the support groups, called them her Fight Club, a reference to the Chuck Palahniuk book (and movie) about people who obsessively attend support groups for the sake of attending support groups. He and I both noted that she'd been there longer than twelve months, which meant she was revisiting the all-important twelve steps. I wondered if that's what codependents were supposed to do. Wasn't the idea that you spent only one year in the group, with the twelve steps coinciding with twelve months, and then, having learned your lessons, you went on with a new and better life, an independent life?

Eventually, the friends she made in the group did just that. They moved on, left the group, possibly overcame their codependency or at least gave it a shot. The plan worked for them. My mom stayed in the group for years, until only she and one other woman were attending. Eventually, they stopped some of the formal meetings and just got together at each other's houses.

Denial is the second aspect that defines my mom's personality. When she learned she had multiple sclerosis, her immediate reaction was to tell no one. It's another resonant moment. She'd married into a greenhouse family where the essence of success was controlling the light, controlling how and when plants grew. Did she think by denying MS, she'd control it? Or at least control who knew about it?

Understanding a few facets of MS sheds light on why my mom sought to deny the disease. The name *multiple sclerosis* means there are multiple unnatural areas of hardened tissues (sclerosis) in the brain or on the spinal cord. How this happens is not entirely known. Doctors have learned that a virus leaps across the blood/brain barrier, attacks helpful T-cells in the immune system, and then morphs the T-cells into aggressive overdrive, causing them to attack sections of nerves. Nerves are normally covered with myelin, but the T-cell attack leads to demyelination. Hard plaques develop on the demyelinated regions, causing telltale symptoms: awkward walking, muscle cramps, fatigue, and loss of balance as the unaffected muscles compensate. The accompanying pain is chronic, acute, and unpredictable, sometimes triggered by food, such as strawberries, or weather, like heat waves.

The origin of the virus, and why it lays dormant for decades, and why many people carry it but never show symptoms, is unknown. Furthermore, MS affects each person differently, and there are four degrees of seriousness, making treatment unpredictable. The lack of a cure, despite decades of research, leads many MS sufferers to apathy, depression, and denial. As their own T-cells destroy nerves, people with MS literally lose their nerve.

My mom was diagnosed in 1996, the summer before my senior year in college. Dad told Matt and me and the grandparents. I was living with a boyfriend near Dayton, so I heard the news over the phone, which made it easy to say *that sucks, I'm sorry, can I do anything, should I come home, No?,* then hang up the phone and continue with my summer of decadence. Now, I regret my selfishness and my own denial.

Mom told no one. For the first three years everything she learned about MS was filtered through what my father read on websites. Mom refused to read about it, to attend support groups or even to reveal new symptoms to the neurologist. If anyone asked why she was walking oddly, she blamed a pulled muscle, or bunions, or that long-ago lawnmower accident that fused her toes. It would be four years before my mom could say *multiple sclerosis* in front of me, and the admission was so significant, I remember it precisely: March 12, 2000, in an evening phone call, as she tearfully told me that Dad was having an affair, and then she said, "This divorce would be easier if I didn't have MS." I was so stunned. She had finally ended 1,460 days of total silence about one of the most significant changes in her life. I wrote it down and even blacked out the square on my calendar and then neither of us mentioned it again for an entire year.

I spent that year pondering how she could only say "MS" in combination with betrayal, as if her MS diagnosis had been one twin lost and wandering, waiting for the other twin disaster to track it down. And my silence echoed more manically than ever. Why had I stubbornly waited for Mom to say the words? I hadn't said them either. I'd made those 1,460 days of total silence worse. No one had blacked out that calendar day but me.

Five years after the diagnosis, she finally told her friends, and slipped notes of explanation into the paycheck envelopes of workers at the greenhouse. At six years, she could look me in the eye and tell me about new treatments and the recent MRI scans of the lesions in her brain, and I could ask questions in return. But she always changed the subject after a few minutes; cowed by those years of easy silence, I let the subject change. At seven years, an activity at Codependents Anonymous required her to write down the mistakes she'd made in her life. "Denying I had MS" topped the list. The other entries dealt almost exclusively with greenhouse decisions. *Giving up floral designing; agreeing to be Alan's secretary.* I know about the list not because I asked, but because I snooped through her paperwork, which I found towering in a disorganized heap on her kitchen table. Silence begets silence, even when you can hear its danger.

It would be nine years before she admitted, directly to me, that denying the diagnosis had been a mistake. She said that at Christmas in 2005, when I started a long conversation about whether or not she could continue to live alone. She said it as a way to assert that she was dealing with her mistakes. I thanked her. But by then, the damage of the silence was done. I doubted there was anything truly redemptive to be said.

My mom's decision to deny she had MS dovetails with codependency. Openly saying she had MS meant she had to take care of herself, a concept foreign to codependents. Her codependency had convinced

Mom and me in the greenhouse, circa 1976

her that the success of Hirt's Greenhouse hinged on her role as book-keeper, and she judged her worth by how others viewed how well the greenhouse was doing. She did not want illness to jeopardize her significance, so she pretended nothing was wrong.

When I think about her level of self-deceit, I'm awestruck by the human mind's capacity to rationalize. She simultaneously saw herself as vital (the bookkeeping job, the status as wife of the owner) yet refused to attend to her physical health, as if the health of her mind (expressed in the upkeep of greenhouse finances) would negate the rapidly failing health of her body.

Essayist Phillip Lopate observed that "We spend most of our adulthoods trying to grasp the meanings of our parents' lives, and how we shape and answer these questions largely turns us into who we are." I'm the poster child for that quote, because by late 2003, I was deep into the final year of a graduate degree, seriously trying to grasp the meaning of my parents' lives. So I went home to Ohio for the holidays and asked my mom to tell me about her role in the greenhouse, starting at the very beginning. Naturally, she started by talking about me, as if I were her beginning.

On February 10, 1975, my mom was nine months pregnant with me. She was twenty-six years old and claims she worked a full eight hours at the greenhouse, helping to prepare for the impending Valentine's Day rush. The next day, she agreed to induce labor so Dad would be free to work for the holiday. Her decision was straight from the textbook of codependency—the needs of Dad and the business took precedent because it would be inconvenient *for other people* if I were born on Valentine's Day. Instead, I came into the world at three in the morning on February 12.

My first stop in this world was not the crib and blankets at home, where a collie-shepherd mix named Sadie would stand sentry. Instead, with three days of life coursing through my eight pounds, my parents drove me to the greenhouse. Cradled in the arms of cooing employees, I bet my eyes tried to focus on the strange expanse of glass, wondering what new womb this was. I've heard that infants have exceptional peripheral vision. I must have seen the greenhouse as a translucent panorama fringed with foliage.

The anecdote, which I heard for the first time two months before my twenty-ninth birthday, pleased me in a way. I was intrigued that Mom had no qualms about taking me to the greenhouse as soon as possible after my birth. I was amused that I'd lived nearly three decades without knowing. Maybe that was why, when I returned to Ohio from my various graduate school residencies, I was compelled to visit the greenhouse first. It had imprinted itself on me.

When my mom recounted her pride at showing me off at the greenhouse, my amazement danced with profound sadness because the aftershocks of the divorce had rendered my mom a *former employee* of Hirt's Greenhouse, the first family member, as far as I knew, to be "let go." And she was let go by none other than her husband, who was also her boss, who was also my father. Mom entering the greenhouse now was taboo, whereas in 1975 she'd been received like a queen bearing the

latest heir. The marriage that allowed her unprecedented access and
status was ending in a divorce that might nullify her claim to the world
under glass.

The event which led to Mom's firing (her word) or being let go
(Dad's phrase) happened in the summer of 2001, a year into the divorce
proceedings. She and Dad had an argument about how to distribute
summer vacation pay bonuses. They were still living together, still
working together. Dad's interpretation of the books showed that the
greenhouse was in debt and the bonus would have to be nixed. Mom's
reading suggested there was leeway for bonuses. It was a tradition. She
knew the employees were counting on the extra money. The argument
dissolved into a no compromise stonewall. When Mom picked up the
phone to get the accountant involved, Dad tried to pull the phone away.
She resisted. When he grabbed her arm, she panicked and dialed 911.
The police dutifully rushed over from their department across the street.
They took a report. Seeing no sign of physical harm to my mom, they
could not press charges against my dad. When the police left, Dad told
Mom to get out. To go home. To stay home. In a decision that confounds
me, she obeyed.

The whole incident was retold in half-truths. Mom amplified the
violence, despite the lack of bruises. Dad amplified Mom's financial
ineptitude, daring to say that the lesions in her brain were affecting her
ability to reason, an unfounded myth of MS. At the time, I was camping
with friends in the Hiawatha National Forest in northern Michigan. I
heard the development, from Mom, when I called to check in. When I
asked the always gut-twisting question "How are you?" she said "I had
to call 911 on your father." The duo of last words stung me unfairly.
Your father. Then she downplayed the fight, making it clear that she wasn't
going to try to press further charges because she was convinced that no
one would believe that her husband of thirty years would suddenly turn
violent. There was, as usual, little I could do, except think about it
constantly on the six-hundred-mile drive south to Ohio. Facing a father
who was also my boss had been hard enough through my teen years.
How in the world was I going to face him now that he had fired my mom
and had maybe tried to physically overcome someone disadvantaged

with MS? And how could I retain any respect for my mother, passively resigned to her situation, now talking as if wives had no rights?

When I returned from the camping trip, Dad's sense of guilt had already kicked in, and he had devised a plan to make himself look better. Rather than flat-out firing Mom, he somehow convinced her to work from home. He set up her computer and desk in my old bedroom. He brought home bookkeeping every day. They agreed she would remain on the payroll, as long as she *worked from home*. Mom accepted the situation. I was relieved that she wouldn't have to exert herself trying to walk around the greenhouse, but the means to that end unsettled me. The situation didn't make sense. The progressive paralysis Mom would face did not need to be accelerated by Dad's plan to keep her at home, symbolically paralyzing her by shutting her off from the other employees. I asked my brother how he and the other employees were reacting to the incident. He said they weren't. No one was talking. I pointed out that Dad would not have dared to grab any other female employee's arm. Matt shrugged. "I'm staying out of it," he said.

Mom had always told me to stand up for myself as a woman. She'd come of age during the feminist movement and had won and kept an elected seat on the previously all-male school board. She'd served on community zoning boards, had led my intrepid Brownie and Girl Scout troops, and had encouraged me to pursue my own interests at college. Her denial of all her problems made little sense. Her public persona and private persona clashed dramatically. I wished she would be honest. Had Dad really hurt her or did she just want to get him in trouble? Her reluctance to pursue charges made me think the 911 call was a bluff. Faced with the dawning realization that I could not fix everything in the few days before I moved to Idaho for graduate school, I stayed silent. I followed my brother's lead: we could, for now, equate silence with neutrality. How keenly aware we were of the danger of picking sides!

On my final night home, I heard the quiet sobs of my mother as she sat at the kitchen table. She was sitting there because Dad had brought home bookwork, but he had left it in the kitchen, not down the hall at her new office. She was no longer coordinated enough to carry it and walk at the same time. She needed to hold on to something—a wall, a chair, Dad's arm—because she had to drag her right leg. She would have benefited from a wheelchair.

Mom thought I was asleep. I soft-stepped across the living room and peered around the corner into the kitchen. I hated to hear her cry, having heard too much of it over the last year. The TV was tuned to Jay Leno, the laughter sometimes covering her sobs, but I saw her shoulders shaking, the tremble of her long blonde hair, hair like mine. She had the greenhouse ledgers opened in front of her, an old adding machine at the ready.

I should have gone to her, should have muted the TV banter. I should have held her hand which refused to bruise. I should have been brave. I should have cried with her. Maybe I was the weak one for *not* crying. How could this family, descended from relatives who raised all this glass, let so many panes slip from the old cypress frames? What could explain this fall from brightest sun to darkest soil, glass shattering on the rims of terracotta, pointing like accusations?

The clarity suggested by growing up surrounded with glass walls is a heady illusion. The walls of the place may as well be black concrete, the airy open stretches really shoulder-tight mazes devoid of logic, even devoid of compassion.

I slipped back into my room when I heard Dad come down the stairs. Since the onset of the divorce, he had taken over the two upstairs rooms, one for a bed, the other for his office. Mom's bedroom remained downstairs. He shuffled into the kitchen, and from my spying spot behind a slightly open door to the guest room, I heard him spew the word *motherfucker* as he apparently pawed through the cupboards, looking for antacids to calm his stomach. He had ulcers.

I was shocked because I'd never heard him use that word. The father whose affection was playfully cloaked in horticultural euphemisms (I was his *little frittilaria*, or, on special occasions, his *tuberose rooted begonia*) was grunting about *all the motherfuckers*. His voice was unusually harsh. I realized he must have been in acute pain to talk like that. *Motherfucker where are the motherfucking pills.* He slammed a cupboard. My heart quaked. Mom calmly directed him to the Tums. I noticed the sudden control in her voice, her sobs seeming to have evaporated. Her tone suggested she was not startled to hear such language. I heard him stomp up the stairs.

I closed the door and locked it. If I hadn't already had plans to leave first thing in the morning, I would have left that instant.

What had I just heard? Dad's ulcers had gotten worse, no doubt. I suspected he had denied his own health problems in order not to worry Mom. I wished he hadn't. I wished he had the confidence to admit he couldn't do everything, couldn't be a husband, a business owner, and a caretaker all at once. And Mom, she straightened up the moment someone needed her, even someone ranting. *"Need yourself!"* I wanted to tell both of them. I felt like I had no idea who these people were.

The next morning I said my farewells, avoiding the gazes and tolerating hugs. I wanted to forget the previous night, to erase the transgression at the greenhouse. There is not much personal pride in my lack of action that summer, but there is honesty. The path of least resistance, of leaving the situation rather than changing it, appealed to me. Interstate 90 put up no fight, and by August, rivers and plains and mountains sat between us.

In 2001, in my new home of Moscow, Idaho, I vowed to figure it all out—the family business, the history of greenhouses, the entire pathology of MS, and just what codependency was—in the process making grand connections about how all these elements got me to where I was.

Ready to confront everything with the flourish and bravado of creativity, I trawled the library with keywords. I read and photocopied. I unabashedly pitched my essays to visiting writers. Hard work would pay off if I just read another book, downloaded one more article, timelined more events. But that moment always remained one step away as I scripted anecdote after anecdote about my relationship with Dad. A professor, commenting on my singular obsession, wrote in the margin, *but where is your mother?*

Where was she? Had I, like my father, deposited her in an oubliette? My dad had always said there was nothing I could do about her MS, nothing would help. *Don't talk to her about it,* he had warned more than once. *The stress of knowing you are worried about her could cause more symptoms.* I began to wonder if I was subconsciously letting his unfounded warning pervade my writing.

One afternoon, I decided to research MS. I found the disease manifests almost exclusively in clustered Caucasian populations north of the equator, with high rates around industrial areas known for pollution. I'd heard that my mom's childhood hometown of Cincinnati, Ohio, was one of these clusters, and I'd heard too that my current home of north Idaho was also an MS cluster. Both cities were on the list, possibly due to their downwind proximity to factories and nuclear power plants. A quick search of the library's catalogue hit on the perfect title: *An Atlas of Multiple Sclerosis*. I trotted upstairs, call number in hand, already imagining maps with little red dots over certain cities, indicating all the empirical evidence I thought was necessary as a doorway into my mother's world.

Previously, I'd skimmed all the other MS books in the library. They proved useless because they were outdated, intended for pre-med students, or cast as lighthearted self-help books with suggestions for maintaining domestic prowess in light of fatigue and crippling pain. (MS afflicts far more women than men.) They offered suggestions like putting rubber bands on doorknobs for ease of turning and using a yardstick to straighten the sheets on the far side of the bed, as if such things should matter when part of your brain is demyelinated. One book listed in detail all the remedies that *didn't* work for alleviating MS symptoms. Not even the work of Nancy Mairs, a talented writer who has MS and writes about it with brashness, bitterness, and maturity, led me to insights about my mother's MS. The title of the *Atlas*, in comparison, seemed promising.

The *Atlas*, however, was page after page of brain scans, brain biopsies, and tissue samples. The language—*note the typical dark-stained periventricular and parenchymatous lesions*—was esoteric. Disappointed, I thumbed through the oversized book anyway, mildly intrigued by the choice of colors applied to brain scans, great clashes of black, red, gold, and green. Then, on page 59, I finally found a geographic map, but it made me want to throw the book across the room.

Figure 22 showed the Hawaiian Islands, their terrestrial tips poking out of the Pacific, their massive underwater bases stretching to the ocean floor. The illustration was simple, with a few shadowy clefts indicating the rugged features. The caption read:

The disease process in multiple sclerosis can be compared with volcanic island chains such as the Hawaiian Islands, where only the tips of the volcanic structures protrude above sea level while unseen activity continues below.

The summer after my fifth-grade year, we'd gone to Hawaii for two weeks, and who knew that it would come back to me this way. What a poor metaphor all around. First, it ripped off the iceberg metaphor into which my mother's *Titanic* was headed. Second, the image was an anomaly in the book, one elementary school illustration within hundreds of pages of brain scans. Third, the comparison wasn't accurate. Lesions were, as far as I understood, flat plaques on nerves, not conical scabs penetrating into the brain. Nor did lesions erupt like the volcano we'd driven half the night to see on that vacation. And the popular image of Hawaii, place of respite and relaxation, when juxtaposed with the "unseen activity" below the water's surface, was just screwy when applied to MS. I was once again amazed, but not surprised to find that research I hoped would enlighten me only annoyed me. I photocopied the page anyway.

Susan Sontag, author of *Illness as Metaphor,* observed that people apply metaphors to illness prior to gaining sound medical facts. For example, before people understood the pathogenesis of cancer, it was commonly believed that repressing desire could lead to tumors, as if the balled-up desire, tucked deep into the netherworld of the body, literally manifested as a ravenous ball of malignant cells. This metaphor was so powerful that it lingers today, stigmatizing the newly diagnosed.

All the unknowns about MS make it a perfect candidate for metaphor. I'm surprised, in fact, that more metaphors don't exist. I partly wish for metaphors, even of the Hawaiian Islands variety. The absence of metaphor is an unnerving silence.

After the telephone incident in the summer of 2001, my mom stopped going to the greenhouse, insisting in a self-deprecating manner that she "wasn't allowed" to cross the threshold, "wasn't allowed" to talk to Dad's parents, "wasn't allowed" to look for another job. I knew her game. Claiming she wasn't allowed was a way to pretend she had no control over her situation.

One time, she called to describe the pretty little violet she'd bought at the grocery store. Then she burst into tears, this woman who once had her free pick of the finest. That's when I knew she was lying to herself, had contrived the light and faked the control.

My brother was aware of her unrelenting distress. He picked out trays of perennials and annuals for her, made mixed bags of bulbs, brought her flower arrangements and a Christmas tree. When my dad left town for a Florida vacation in December 2003, Matt invited Mom up to the greenhouse, "because Dad's not around." I was visiting too, and the plan thrilled me because my brother recognized how much the greenhouse meant to Mom.

That afternoon, she needed close to forty-five minutes to walk the length of the main greenhouse, down to the end where Matt wanted to show her a rare red passionflower in bloom. I circled around, snapping pictures, nervously watching my mom as she tottered with a black cane on the wet greenhouse floor. Employees came out to say hi, to say they missed her, to tell me I was all grown up now, to assure Mom that Matt was keeping things together in this old greenhouse. No one mentioned Dad; no one mentioned MS. We talked about coffee plants and henna plants which were a huge hit on eBay, about the massive Boston fern whose roots had cracked right through the plastic pot, about the varie-gated clivia houseplant sprout Matt had nurtured from seed and slapped a fifty-dollar price tag on after he researched the its rarity. The sprout was maybe an inch tall, with two green and white striped leaves.

"Fifty dollars?" I asked him.

"I guarantee you'll never see a variegated clivia again," he said, cocky and grinning. He later asked me if I wanted to get in on the greenhouse lottery pool. He was incredulous when I told him I never played the lottery.

Mom worked her way back out of the greenhouse, casting comments about how "Dad has really let this place run-down." I halfway agreed, but I hesitated when I caught myself fixating on the rings on her hands.

My brother, Matt, and Mom, December 2003

My mom had always displayed about seven gemstones—diamonds, amethysts, sapphires, emeralds, and turquoise—on gold bands or set in silver. Her long nails were still somehow manicured. She probably had a couple thousand dollars worth of rocks on her fingers, and one was probably her wedding ring. I realized that in all my years at the greenhouse, I'd never seen her hands dirty, never saw her carry a tray of plants or wrestle with a heavy wet hose. She'd always sat in her air-conditioned office, wearing a silk or faux-silk shirt, counting the money, tapping totals on the keyboard. Everything, the rare clivia, my snubbing of the lottery, my mother's rings, was suddenly speaking to me of *status*, an awareness so ingrained in me, Jen Hirt, whose family owned Hirt's Greenhouse, that I hadn't ever recognized it. We were all so status-conscious, so unable to see the greenhouse for the glass. The struggle to maintain that status was like the old Boston fern cracking its own pot in hunger for more water, more sun.

I have only one metaphor for MS. At the greenhouse, all of us in the family faced severe "role confusion," a term noted in various business books as one of the unique problems encountered by family businesses. In a family business, knowing when to act like an employee or a family member can be impossible to decode. Wife or secretary? Daughter or clerk? Owner or brother? Son or manager-in-training? No clear lines are ever drawn. Roles get confused and stay confused for decades, undermining morale.

In my mother's body, the T-cells also confused their roles. Rather than helping her immune system, they overreacted and attacked parts of her nervous system, like viruses. Currently, she injects herself with Copaxon to temper the T-cells, to remind them of their confusion. The injections seem to work. The MS is still progressing, but has been slowed.

In late 2007, when she let slip in a conversation that she was buying her groceries at Walgreens because the supermarkets were too exhausting to navigate, even with the motorized carts, I signed her up for an in-home help service that shopped for groceries and did light cleaning. She didn't want to do it. I insisted.

A few weeks in, I called to see how things were going. She'd already paid for two weeks of the service but hadn't used it once. She said she hadn't sent her helper shopping yet because she didn't know if the helper would know where things were in the grocery store. I pointed out that someone hired specifically to do grocery shopping could certainly be trusted. In the silence on the phone I could hear her trying to think of a reason why she was the only person who could shop for her own groceries. And in that moment I wondered if years of counseling at Codependents Anonymous had done anything for her. She could talk their talk; she had the library of self-help books. She could spot the tendency in others. But she couldn't take the essential steps to let other people help her.

In that moment of silence, I remembered that when I was sixteen and she sent me grocery shopping for the first time, she'd put the items in order of the aisles. In her world, you couldn't just shop for groceries at random. You had to get them in order. I realize now she treated everyone exactly like that. She thought she had to do everything, down to advising me how to navigate the aisles, right foot in front of left, and then left in front of right.

But now, she had forgotten the order of the aisles. Her old grocery store was long closed, and the new ones were foreign territory. That's why she couldn't make a list. And if she couldn't make a list, she couldn't send her helper shopping.

Eureka! I had spotted the one remaining obstacle. It was like I had grabbed the last clump of troublesome leaves that prevented water from draining from the gutter. Only it wasn't just leaves. It was something odd, an anomaly, a giant walnut tucked away by a misguided squirrel, or a wad of duct tap blown in from a storm, or anything else random and in the wrong place. You clear the gutter, both amused and horrified by the strange thing causing the problem, and water drains out in an obedient rush, finally going where it's supposed to go.

So I told her stories of all the times I'd moved to a new town with new grocery stores and new layouts. I had managed. I hinted at how much better she'd feel if she ate regular meals again. She agreed. We talked through a list that prioritized the food she wanted, rather than a list that baby-stepped the helper through the aisles. I reassured her ten times that the order of the list didn't matter as long as she got the staples she needed.

A few days later, she called. She was ecstatic. She'd made a grocery list for that week's helper, a young man, and he'd successfully returned with all the items, neatly bagged, neatly checked off, her change in an envelope. He put away her groceries and made her a light lunch consisting of cold cuts, cheese cubes, and fresh fruit. He chatted with her while she ate, and they watched Oprah. *"I didn't know men could shop!"* she said when she called me with the story. It was a revelation.

Into the Teeth of It

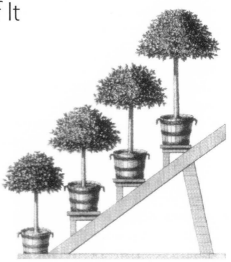

Here's a revelation of my own: In the midst of researching greenhouses, I discovered a new bloodline of sorts. I found that as my family fell apart, I was eager to bind outsiders to my heritage, to make them mine. Enter American poet Theodore Roethke.

One day in graduate school, a professor put a photocopied poem in my mailbox. The first lines were: *where were the greenhouses going, / lunging into the lashing / wind driving water / so far down the river.* The poem was "Big Wind" by Roethke. He had been a third-generation member of his family's greenhouse business in Saginaw, Michigan, in the 1920s.

The Roethkes grew flowers for florists' shops, long beds of roses, chrysanthemums, and carnations. "Big Wind" imagined their greenhouses as old ships caught in a fierce storm, the workers sheltered inside with the precious cargo of roses. They watched the glass crack, heard the framework groan against the wind, until *she rode it out, / that old rose-house, / she hove into the teeth of it, / the core and pith of that ugly storm.* I read it and thought of my grandpa's long-dead brother, Paul, who died when the *Otranto* sank. If only the *Otranto* could have ridden it out like Roethke's rose house.

Roethke wrote fourteen poems about his greenhouses. They traced the cycle of greenhouse life, from the rose bush struggling to set root to the dissident flower blooming on the compost pile. One of Roethke's biographers, Neal Bowers, noted that "Roethke's greenhouse is the ultimate symbol of growth, a 'womb of cypress and double glass.'" The growth struggle, as witnessed by the imaginative mystic Roethke, provided "an exact parallel for the spirit in its struggle to rise to a new level of reality."

To come across Roethke's poems at the time I did was fortuitous. Here was the Famous American Poet, dead before I was born, yet we'd both seen what the other had seen. I considered the coincidence that he had written fourteen greenhouse poems, and in Ohio, my family had built fourteen greenhouses over the years. But what really mattered was that Roethke was as much an ancestor as my grandparents or great-grandparents. Discovering his poems was like discovering a new heritage.

In a 1953 essay about his poetry, Roethke explained what the green-houses meant to him.

They were to me, I realize now, both heaven and hell, a kind of tropics created in the savage climate of Michigan, where austere German Americans turned their love of order and their terrifying efficiency into something truly beautiful. It was a universe, several worlds, which, even as a child, one worried about, and struggled to keep alive.

Roethke's universe was mine, too. He cast into lyric what I had observed—the gritty underworld of roots, the slick algae-rich corners where glass met cement, the riotous blooms and foliage. There was the quiet world of the plants, whose daylong activity might be pushing aside a clump of soil, in contrast with the hustle of workers dragging cantan-kerous hoses, hoisting trays and baskets to the sun-filled heights, and smoothing money into the black dividers of the cash register. As a child

in my greenhouses, I could run from the South House, with its cacti
jutting from sand, to the North House, dank and clustered with jungle
growth, then on to the larger greenhouse where familiar and foreign
aromas evanesced from ferny herbs, finally skipping to a halt in the
lavish Flower House, a gift store with Mylar balloons and a walk-in cooler
of cut flowers. Or there was the world of my grandfather, who, as he
doddered toward senility, spent far too much time nurturing trays of
moss, compared to the world of my father, who jettisoned the greenhouse
to small-town stardom with his TV appearances and radio show.

Where I differ from Roethke is in the realm of play and privilege.
Whereas he was subject to the strict work ethic of his elders, noting in
his journals that "I was born under a glass heel and have always lived
there," I was born onto a glass pedestal.

Being the daughter of the owner, I spent my childhood hanging out
at the greenhouse, which was located about ten miles away from our
rural home. As an infant, I accompanied my parents to work. My crib
was in the office where my mom took flower orders, where my uncle
laid out plans for spring vegetable plantings, where my dad tallied
Christmas sales, where my grandpa worried about humidity levels for
his prized African violets, where my grandmother tagged perennials
with their Latin names, a task she accomplished from memory, with
perfect spelling and sleek cursive. Two years later, my brother, Matt,
burbled in the crib. I like to think I toddled around the place, one hand
on someone's knee, the other gripping the nearest leaf.

We played so thoroughly at the greenhouse, Matt and I. More than
half the time we were probably fighting or plotting to get each other in
trouble, but still, the memories are irrepressibly fond. The place was
huge, sun-drenched, housing a peculiar echo of voices off glass. Today,
the unmistakable scent of wet soil still vortexes me back to the center
of growth. Long aisles crowded with plants were perfect for tag and
other pursuits. Roethke called them alleys, and wrote about his father
lifting him up so he could see down the narrow rows of tall rose bushes,
their red buds crowning into the evening dusk. Damp corners proved
peerless for staring at moss and snails. Mountains of bagged mulch out
back were unequaled for climbing and jumping. Battery-powered

Stomper 4 x 4 trucks, all the rage in the '80s, encountered Herculean
trials as my brother and I set them on courses traversing complicated
arrays of soil, pots, and sticks. When the batteries drained, we folded
paper airplanes from greenhouse stationery, or lapsed into our favorite pastime, a two-person hide-and-seek-and-tag game. Our greatest
secret, our private delight, was a population of chameleons who skit-
tered through trays of ivy, daring us to hunt them, catch them, carry
them in jars. To top it off, our dog trotted at our heels, her chain collar
glinting the sun and her wolfish tail wagging against steam pipes. These
adventures were the privilege of privileged children, and we knew it.

Roethke, I think, would have longed to fit right in with us. We were
little lords of our tropical kingdom, oblivious to the boundary between
workplace and play place, rarely chastised for our exuberance, which
often resulted in tipped pots or broken stems. Roethke, like my father,
was probably not allowed to play in the greenhouse. For those generations, work held priority. And yet he must have trembled over the possibilities of the sublime greenhouse world, the way it begged exploration.
Roethke captured it all in his poem "Child on Top of a Greenhouse."

The wind billowing out the seat of my britches,
My feet crackling splinters of glass and dried putty,
The half-grown chrysanthemums staring up like accusers,
Up through the streaked glass, flashing with sunlight,
A few white clouds all running eastward,
A line of elms plunging and tossing like horses,
And everyone, everyone pointing up and shouting!

I fully believe Roethke climbed up on a greenhouse at some point
in his life, just to prove he could do it. His moxie makes me smile. What
aggressive energy, what skill, what a drive to see things from a different
perspective. What subtle pleasure at subverting the daily routine, at
shattering the glass heel he felt he was under. For every hour I literally
spent playing on the wonderfully dirty floor of the greenhouse, there
have been two hours where I've been that child on top of a greenhouse,
the whole place my pedestal. Stare up and accuse me, half-grown chrysanthemums.

Eventually, play dissolved into work, a change I embraced because it meant I was growing up. Like all the branches in the family tree, I was a part-time employee of Hirt's Greenhouse, starting when I was fifteen, ending when I was twenty-three.

However, I wasn't like the other clerks. No application, no interview, no training period. I didn't eat lunch at the chipped table in the windowless break room. I was allowed lunch money from petty cash, and then I'd drive to some fast food place, come back, and perch in my dad's chair in the air-conditioned office, listening to Pearl Jam and enjoying the view from the wallwide window that faced the interior of the largest greenhouse. I didn't have to park around back. I left my new blue Chevy Beretta next to my dad's red Toyota MR2, which was next to my mom's evergreen Dodge Stealth, and eventually my brother's turquoise Ford Ranger. I was in the privileged parking area. My car insurance was paid through the greenhouse's policy. I drove the Beretta for eight years and never once saw a monthly payment slip, not one insurance premium, and there was always easy cash for gas.

Nor was I mired in the standard eight-hour shift. Sometimes, I'd ride with my dad in one of the Hirt's Greenhouse vans, painted with our name and a bundle of roses, to pay a visit to a wholesale greenhouse. I'd help him load huge palms sleeved in brown paper. I ran errands for Mom. I picked up the payroll, banked checks and cash, remembered Dad's shirts at the dry cleaner's, bought burgers and fries for lunch.

Finally, I had access. I cashed out the drawers at night, often counting a thousand in currency. I had a key to the filing cabinet that served as the safe, and I had a tiny key to the petty cash box. In fact, I had a key ring as cumbersome as my dad's with keys to the front doors, the side doors, the back door, the office door, to all the padlocks on all the gates of the chain-linked nursery area, all six cash registers, and a square key to the old fake-wood-paneled Pepsi machine which often jammed. Freedom not for the average teenage clerk. Freedom because of my last name and lineage.

Behind the cash register I realized I harbored no inclinations for customer service, which was the job I performed most often at the greenhouse. I was shy and anxious, constantly averting my eyes behind long bangs. I was short. I was terrified of making a mistake involving money. I was troubled because I didn't know the answers to all the questions. I longed for a job watering the quiet rows of ferns with the heavy hose and water wand (a long metal extension for reaching the hanging plants), a tool guaranteed to keep the customers at least five feet back. But only my dad and uncle watered, because they too were not fond of being stuck at the cash register for an eight-hour shift.

My dad was a terror at customer service. It was us versus them when it came to fielding complaints, concerns, or even just assisting a little old lady who couldn't find the parsley. Countless times, I saw him act needlessly rude for his own entertainment. When someone complained about not finding the tomatoes, he told them to go to one of the discount stores if it was so hard. He hung up on callers. He ordered people out promptly at closing time, turning off the lights while reminding them he'd been there for eight hours and just wanted to sit on the couch for a while, and was that too much to ask?

I inherited his animosity genes, but not his rudeness. Customers, whom I found exceedingly annoying without exception, caused me anxiety. To quell the anxiety, I negated them—no eye contact, no conversation, just the exchange of money, the tendering of the receipt, and a hollow "*Have a nice day.*" When there weren't any customers, I'd escape. I'd use my square vending machine key to get a free Pepsi, and I'd wander off into the rows of plants, completely content to examine their leaves, to admire how their stems arched, to envy their silence and perfection.

Roethke too negated the actual human presence in nearly half of his fourteen poems about greenhouses, but he cleverly used greenhouse imagery to represent human emotions (without ever including many humans). Scholar George Wolff, in his biography of Roethke, noted Roethke's inclusion and exclusion of family members in his memories of the greenhouse. Wolff concluded

Clearly, the absence of human beings is more striking than their presence... The quality of life the plants experience reflects the quality of the emotional and spiritual life of the poet.

When I first read that analysis, recognition hit, just like with "Big Wind." I'd found the next piece of glass in the new greenhouse. I began to understand. *"The quality of life the plants experience reflects the quality of the emotional and spiritual life of the poet."*

At our greenhouses, the quality of life for the plants was good but brief. Growing plants was a goal, but selling them quickly was the real goal. The faster they moved from the benches, the fewer waterings they required. Water is a major expense in a greenhouse, so profits spike when plants move quickly off the benches. The longer the plants stay, the more water they need, the more fertilizer, bigger pots, and more space. When they finally sell, the profit is scant, lost in their upkeep. Almost ninety years of success means that countless plants have spent just a few weeks at Hirt's before moving on to gardens and living rooms. The success of Hirt's isn't just dependent on workers having the knowledge to grow stuff. Customers must have the desire to buy. As a clerk, I rang up hundreds of plants a day, bagged them and boxed them, sent them away as merchandise. For eight hours I stood at that transition point, the area, literally, where the quality of life changed.

Looking back, I recall worrying that the customers would not take proper care of the plants. I even created a file of care sheets and passed them out with each purchase, intent on educating people. But in the background I'd hear my dad arguing on the phone, or just slamming it down, frustrated with another stupid customer. I'd see my mom sitting at the desk next to him, keeping the books, recording the only really important transactions—how the plants became profit. I eyed each customer with suspicion, as if few were worthy.

As the teenage clerk, I didn't always make the smartest decisions, nor was I overly polite, but then again, these were traits hardly unusual given my age. But once, on a Sunday morning when I alone had opened the greenhouse and was manning the whole place until my parents arrived later, I ran out of quarters for change for an old man who seemed disappointed that the only employee around was a girl who couldn't tell him anything about the mineral needs of orchids, which we didn't sell anyway. By this time, I'd realized it was okay to say *"I don't know,"* and most customers understood, offering to come back later when my dad was around. The old guy bought something insignificant and paid with a fifty. The necessary change tapped my tens, then my fives, then my dollar bill and quarter reservoir. I counted out his remaining change in small coins. I dropped the handful of change into his palm. The disappointment of his whole wasted visit to the greenhouse welled up in his throat, and he spat at me, "What's this?"

"I don't have enough quarters," I said, probably in an inappropriate tone.

"Well go get some. I don't want all these pennies."

I said *no*. Plain old *no*. The *no* of the well-off kid who had it rough because she had to work on a Sunday. The *no* I'd been saying for years, the self-centered mantra *no*, the *never* of every pseudo-rebellious rock-song I sang in the brand new car my parents bought for my sweet sixteen. There were quarters, probably, but I didn't want to go through the *trouble*, the *hassle*, of getting them out of the petty cash box. I didn't give a shit if he didn't want to carry around coins. It was his fault for paying with a fifty. He was a rude old man, the epitome of the bad customer, bothering me on a Sunday morning. It wasn't my problem. The phone rang and I turned my back to him, forgot him. When I hung up and turned back around, he threw the change at me, side-arming it against the countertop so it shot back up at my chest in a wide spray. He left immediately, before I could compose a reaction, not that I knew what to do anyway, and besides, I was alone. I picked up every coin.

It was a startling moment, an incident of resentment against my rudeness. "No" was my default answer to many requests by authority figures, and no one had ever challenged me on it. I was edgy for a few hours, worried he'd come back, then I fumed for days. The nerve of that geezer, chucking his change at me, one of the *Hirts*. It had to have been formative, that morning alone in the greenhouse, me failing magnificently and blaming the customer, as if nothing were ever my fault. I was my dad's daughter to the core. Yet in a way, the troublesome customers were almost a rite of passage into the way I saw my father do business.

I so loathed customers that I got to the point where, during the spring sale of vegetable three-packs and twelve-pack flats, I memorized

Corner of my grandparents' private greenhouse, winter 2002

the price with tax for the common combinations (such as two full flats) so that I wouldn't have to waste a few extra seconds waiting for the cash register to tally the total. It was the busiest time, the most stressful, with customers crowding the aisles, sometimes arguing over the last pack of heirloom tomatoes or Dutch hybrid peppers. We were open for thirteen hours a day. I'd have four or five customers in line at all times, and I'd look back through the line and tick off their totals for them so by the time they got up to the counter, they'd have their checks signed or their cash or credit ready. I was speedy. No small talk. No pleasantries. Automatic for the people, the people who were just taking up too much space. Get them in and out, have it over and done with. The greenhouses of sprouts were emptied by June, as if the plants grew on a conveyor belt running from the steamy back corners to the parking lot.

Thinking back on my few years of tenure at that cash register, I realize I thought highly of my aloofness, my tax-calculating skills, and my place in the hierarchy of the family business. I deserved to be taken down a notch, although the old guy's method backfired stupendously and no one else stepped up to the challenge, not even my parents.

The problem was that I wanted the greenhouse to be more than it was. I imagined it as a conservatory, a botanical garden, a royal hideaway with the rarest plants. I resented the customers because their presence meant they would carry off a plant I had been contemplating for days. But Hirt's needed customers to stay in business. I didn't have a mind for business. Neither did Roethke.

In his poem "Moss Gathering," Roethke describes collecting moss from a nearby wetland and carrying it back to the greenhouses, where it was probably used in bedding, packing, or mulching. He wrote,

And afterwards I always felt mean, jogging back over the logging road,
As if I had broken the natural order of things in that swampland;
Disturbed some rhythm, old and of vast importance,
By pulling off flesh from the living planet;
As if I had committed, against the whole scheme of life, a desecration.

The greenhouse's simulation of the scheme of life resonated with that tenor of desecration, oddly enough. All these plants in cheap plastic pots were for the convenience of customers, not so much for the needs of the plants. Stock which stayed too long often ended up in the trash. And here was my self, my being. As a child I had contributed my own youthful rhythm of play to the rhythm of life in a greenhouse. Those days were wonderful. I begged to go to the greenhouse. As a teen, the rhythm shifted to a workday, to a paycheck, to sore feet and more money than I could comprehend as the plants passed through my hands as commodities. I longed for closing time, for days off. The more I worked at the greenhouse, the more I wanted to get away from it, *"as if I had committed, against the whole scheme of life, a desecration."*

When I moved to Moscow, Idaho, for graduate school, my dad called one afternoon and requested I send him "liverworts, mosses, lichens. Unusual stuff from the forests out there." He told me to toss the plants in a box and ship them UPS overnight, and he would try to cultivate them for bonsai use. A few days later, friends and I hiked in the St. Joe National Forest. The cedar-shadowed terrain was spongy with colonies of mosses. I'd never seen so many varieties. But I couldn't bring myself to divot them from the woodland floor.

I was thinking of Roethke's moss-gathering poem, of course, but also so much more. On my knees, I peered intently at their miniature worlds. Amber moss stamens five-pointed into green stars. They were galaxies, exploding and static all at once. I brushed my hand over their softness, unrivaled. A friend was raving about the wonders of imperceptibly slow growth, insisting that lichen grew maybe a centimeter a year on rocks, and wasn't that amazing, that tenacity? I listened to her and knew she was right. I heard Roethke, from a journal entry I'd been contemplating the night before, whispering *"star-flower, portal into the night, / breathing brighter than water, / the twilight cannot whelm you."* I pictured the lovely moss dried out and battered in a box in the belly of a UPS cargo plane. I foresaw my dad patting the moss onto soil around pseudo-bonsai trees, which were really just young juniper sprigs trimmed artfully and plunked into decorative bowls. *The trees are breathing less. / You, winky, sleep. / I've come to tear the sun out. / Save me, mouse.*

I never sent the moss. Never even pulled it from the forest.

And although it took me a long time, I understand now that I have no regrets about leaving the family business to the business-minded.

Cut

This urge, wrestle, resurrection of dry sticks,
Cut stems struggling to put down feet,
What saint strained so much,
Rose on such lopped limbs to a new life?
    —Theodore Roethke

We were a longhaired family for the longest time. We resisted any suggestion of *cutting*. My mother had bleached-blonde hair down her back, bangs cut straight, an even, clean part at all times. She never braided, never pulled her hair away from her face or off her neck. She owned no barrettes, no clips. My dad had a brown curly mess most of the time, loose and spilling into a thick brief beard. He rarely wore hats; sometimes a sweatband to lift the curls off his forehead. They were mainstream hippies whose closets held leather fringe, unworn since the early seventies, when they were twenty-somethings eager to assume ownership of the greenhouse.

A generation later, my brother let his thick blond-brown hair fall past his shoulders. As for me, who has had major haircuts exactly ten times in her life, I feel like my hair should be longer, should not taper down my back but cover it, fall past both hips like a cape, as if every hair from every year should still be with me. Yet hair is dead to begin with, and my hair will never grow longer. An average strand remains four years, growing six inches a year, before the follicle dies. New follicles open, replace, and inherit so steadily that it seems like my hair never changes, never succumbs.

I used to do this: about once a month, I would sit for hours with sharp scissors and clip split ends, thinking *this time I'll get them all*. I never did.

❊❊❊❊

Families name us and define us, give us strength, give us grief. All our lives we struggle to embrace or escape their influence. They are magnets that both hold us close and drive us away.
—George Howe Colt

My parents' divorce is something I continually return to, not unlike the way I compulsively return to the split ends. Vigilance, in hindsight with words or in the moment with scissors, quells concern, however temporary and fleeting.

Somewhere in the midst of years worth of complicated court proceedings, while they fought bitterly over rights to the family's greenhouse business and the rights to our home in the woods of Valley City, Ohio, my dad shaved the beard he'd worn for twenty-five years and wrapped his hair in a tight thin ponytail that looked like some sort of lonesome root. He withdrew thousands from his retirement account, paying for laser surgery to remove all the hair on his back.

My mom, her hair unchanged for decades, had her sister lop it off to shoulder length on a Thanksgiving evening. It was a strange cut, straight across, as if done in a hurry, as if the fingers curled in the circles of the scissors were angry yet ready for a change.

My brother moved out of the house my parents were fighting over and as far as I know, hasn't cut his hair since.

And me?

❊❊❊❊

Three months after my parents hired lawyers and announced their intentions to embark on a split that would consume the next few years, they dutifully drove 750 miles together to attend my graduation from a master's program at Iowa State University. They traveled together

Self-portrait in the South House, winter 2003

because my mom's paralysis had taken root in her right side. She couldn't negotiate the clutch of their stick-shift and hadn't driven in years anyway. A lack of forethought negated plane tickets. The manual car was, in fact, the most inappropriate car for the semi-handicapped—a racy Dodge Stealth, low-slung and shaped for speed, with sleek slanted seats she had to slide into. But part of my mom's denial included pretending she did not wish to drive anymore, and she double-denied by supposing a marathon road trip across the Midwest with her estranged husband would be appropriate, a grand idea, not a problem at all.

The entire graduation weekend was a ridiculous and horribly wrong tumble through a domestically dark pretend world. We hugged tentatively and spoke cautiously in complete sentences, for fear of being misunderstood. We said nothing of substance. We spoke, but our mouths never moved. Mom and Dad asked me about Iowa, about job prospects, about my boyfriend, Paul, a year behind me in graduate school. They did not speak to each other unless necessary. I answered their questions and bit my lips, stuck on a childhood lesson from *Peter Cottontail* and *Bambi*. "If you don't have anything nice to say, don't say anything at all."

Somehow, we tolerated each other through restaurant meals and tours around campus, gliding to the graduation ceremony on the ethers of Midwest repression. I crossed the stage holding an empty diploma cover, not yet cleared to receive the real degree for a few weeks. One more sham, but why not? In the audience were my parents, side by side—but the farthest apart they'd ever been. Of course they insisted on a family picture, and I let down my defenses, telling myself to be thankful that they cared enough about me to bother. We lined up in the dusky red of the auditorium, Dad, Mom, and me. Mom stood in between so she wouldn't fall. Her balance was nearly nonexistent, and she dragged her right leg. The muscles around her ankle joint and knee joint had long ago ceased negotiations with her brain, and the hip joint was considering the same. She desperately needed a cane, a walker, a wheelchair, but insisted upon holding my dad's arm, almost all the time, even after she knew of his infidelity. She tried to make her disability a reason for matrimony at all costs.

In the picture, she is leaning into my dad, and he has tentatively, unbelievably, *what does he think he's trying to pull off,* placed his hand on her shoulder. But I realize, too, that by leaning into him for support, my mom is just as manipulative, if not more. The longer she cradles her arm in his, the more pictures we take this way, and the more their physical union is proven on Kodak, the less chance he has of really leaving.

I'm present but I'm not. There is space between my mother and me, and my mother is the space between my father and me. Hidden and proud, desperate to escape in my sleek black robe, I lean ever so slightly away, as if betrayal and denial are contagious.

Weeks later, when I saw the picture, I was struck by how nice my hair looked. Damn long, shimmering in the static moment, hanging down the front of my robe like the golden honor society cords I'd never earned. Maybe it was the light, or the contrast against my black robe, or maybe I saw what I wanted to see. My mother's hair was the usual lemon white, ethereal after decades of constant coloring, hard to delineate against the pastel yellow jacket she wore over a white shirt. She looked like a tepid sun, and me in my black robe, I was a universe stretching faster than the speed of light, faster than the speed of black. I was one atomic shudder away from playgrounding comets, if only I could survive this photo shoot with my parents. Dad was a terrestrial planet, a darker distant Earth in his jeans and gray-green shirt, almost cut loose from the obligation of orbit. We were a shaky universe.

The day after my parents left, unaware that I would be vainly impressed by a picture yet to arrive, I walked into We Care Hair and asked the stylist to cut off whatever looked bad.

❀❀❀❀

Our greenhouses in Ohio used to have a series of long low cold frames. They were about four feet high, thirty feet long, with peaked roofs and the standard panes of glass. They were designed, in miniature, to conserve heat. We used them to start the cold weather vegetables, such as cabbage, broccoli, and peas. The roofs were vented to keep the frost out at night. Entire panes of glass were hinged onto a frame and could be cranked wide open. The only way in and out of the old cold frames was through the vents.

One summer night, after the cold weather vegetables sold out, a terribly confused young doe crashed through one of the cold frames. Where she was headed, what she thought she saw, what she assumed she was jumping into, no one knew. My brother and I, we must have been six and eight, peered at the doe through glass while the grownups debated. She had gigantic ears. It was no less than magic that she was in our greenhouse. She had to have been injured. There was blood on the broken glass of the cold frame and the dagger shards lay all around her. But no one could see cuts, and clearly she was alive and alert, curled neatly on the sandy floor, like a figurine. Worried that she would panic, crash back out, and dart into the traffic of the nearby intersection, my dad called Animal Control. An officer responded and had to deal not only with the deer but with my mother, who said, kids in mind, the deer would not be shot, no matter how serious the injury, no matter how strange the predicament. Not at her greenhouse.

The next morning, my mom told me a fabulous story about how at midnight, my dad slowly cranked open the vents, and the brave deer stood, jumped, and the moon was full and everyone watched her trot down the road before she bounded into a small patch of woods. It was easy to believe, to believe that all cuts healed themselves, that panic had no consequences, and survival triumphed this time.

❀❀❀❀

For every kind of vampire, there is a kind of cross.
—Thomas Pynchon

In the many mirrors of We Care Hair, where everyone asked if I'd ever seen Crystal Gale's hair (yes), I glanced with caution at the stylist. Her name was mine, Jennifer, which I decided was a good sign. She slid my most reliable gray scrunchie down my ponytail and said for the entire salon to hear, "*Damn,* your hair is *long.*" Jennifer brushed it out and nodded like a mechanic diagnosing a major engine problem. "Oh *yeah,* your ends are split *real* bad. This all needs to go."

This all. The imprecision of her quantification was somehow convincing. An elaborate mirror set-up allowed me to see the back of my head while looking forward. She was pointing to a cut line about six inches higher than my frazzled, thin ends, ends which brushed the belt loops on my jeans. It would be the most hair I had ever had cut. *This needs to happen,* I told myself. *Hair grows back.*

She swiveled the chair slightly, obscuring my view. She got down on her knees and brushed my hair straight. Her scissors were so quiet.

❀❀❀❀

My grandpa's brother was in WWII. He kept a fabulous scrapbook of his service time in India, including photos, letters, newspaper clippings, money, even chopsticks taped onto a page. The scrapbook lay in an attic for decades, until I reclaimed it one summer when my dad was cleaning out his parents' house.

There are two bizarre postcards just a few pages in. They are a series. In the first postcard, a young black bull is rigged to a post with ropes lashed across his back, head and horns. The ropes run through a hole in the post, and off-picture, I imagine strong men are leaning against the ropes, forcing the bull's forehead against the post. Behind him, four men hold more ropes and his tail. The bull's muscles are braced and strained like the ropes. His eyes are planets. On the right, a lithe young man is on tiptoe, his torso stretching up out of the frame. I can see a crescent of his face, his eyes focused on the narrowest part of the bull's neck. I realize what he's wielding above his head, out of the frame. My eyes drop to the second postcard.

The head is severed, falling, not yet on the ground. There is a spray of black blood—surprisingly, not much. The innards of the bull's neck are white and clear and alive. Blood hasn't had time to gush from the huge wound. The photographer caught the split second when the blood did not yet know of the cut, when the hindquarters did not realize they could cease straining to escape. The cleanness of the cut is notable. The spine is severed neatly. The man with the scimitar, knife, machete, whatever it is, is in a full crouch, the momentum forcing him to his heels. The men behind the bull have shut their faces in deep squints. Perhaps they have seen this beheading before. Perhaps no one can really watch such a fatal cut in real time. Perhaps that's why there are postcards.

❀ ❀ ❀ ❀

When I was ten, my family visited Cancun, Mexico. The black-haired Mexican servers at the hotel's buffet nearly fell over themselves to carry my plates back to the table. They did the same for my blond little brother, and often for my mom, but never for my brown-haired dad. Mom whispered, "They like blond hair."

I contemplated this. It was just hair. Or was it? All I wanted was a second bowl of seafood soup, not an entourage of Mexican men escorting me back and forth because of my hair. I was too young for this. I was uncomfortable. Mexican men adored my hair, yet my parents had warned me constantly to be wary of strangers (and for a girl from Ohio, Mexican men exemplified *strangers*). During the trip, my dad insisted that we swallow antibiotics three times a day, "because of the water," which reinforced the notion that the place was dangerous, that the Mexicans were reservoirs of bacteria, to be avoided but tolerated whenever we left the sparkling resort courtyard. These realities, filtered through my young perception of *foreign*, clashed with the swell of pride in my mom's voice when she explained the actions of the buffet attendants. Her tone, the smile in her eyes, suggested I should be pleased, honored, and proud.

I had the advantage of long blonde *American* hair. When I think back on it now, I'm appalled by that pride in my mother's voice.

During that Mexican vacation, we visited Mayan ruins. On one outing, my brother and I climbed the temples of Tulum, delighting in the views of the ocean and the roll of waves mixed with foreign words. We were wowed by the stories of human sacrifice, the cutting and offering of beating hearts. On the beach, where the empire fell away to the shoreline, my brother and I played in the surf. We were distracted by an almond-brown boy posing for pictures with a weird little pet. I remember the pet as a guinea pig with an anteater nose and a prehensile tail. The boy let me hold the animal. Mom snapped a picture as I petted the strange thing, which was a thousand times cooler than my Ohio menagerie of rabbits, hamsters, and cats.

Then the boy held my elbow and waved to his family. He wanted a picture with *me*. He slid his hand down the back of my head, cupped his fingers against my neck, spread his palm between my shoulder blades, and let his hand slide all the way down the entire length of my hair, slightly wet and stringy, gone white with salt and sun, as exotic to him as his pet was to me. I froze, and the boy pressed his hand harder against my back, daring to feel the slip of strands in the flex of his palm.

❊❊❊❊

Last night the apple tree shook and gave each lettuce a heart
Six hard red apples broke through the greenhouse glass and
Landed in the middle of those ever-so-slightly green leaves
That seem no mix of seeds and soil but pastels and light and
Chalk x's mark our oaks that are supposed to be cut down
  —Matthea Harvey

My teen requests to get my hair permed, or highlighted, *something* other than the plain longness of it all, met with stubborn resistance from my mom. "Trust me," she said, "You don't want a permanent."

"Mom, it's called a *perm*, not a *permanent*." I was mortified by the ongoing social embarrassment of parents.

My best friend Heidi had long, blonde, permed hair, and the bouncy style smothered me with envy. Heidi was the typical best friend. She was popular, listened to all the right music, bought stylish clothes, and had a boyfriend. Even her lunches seemed more mature. She ate oatmeal crème cookies and ham sandwiches, compared to my peanut butter and jelly on white bread, with animal crackers in a baggie. She had done something nice with her hair; the spirals were light and long. My straight heavy hair matted at the nape of my neck. Mousse and hairspray were useless. It grew oily every day and I felt embarrassed to have to wash it so much. I tried pigtails and ponytails and braids, but succeeded only in messy, tangled hairdos, something the other girls seemed never to encounter. The secret of junior high hair eluded me.

But at the mercy of my mom for money and transportation and approval, there was little I could do when she said "no" to a perm. I resorted to putting my wet hair into twenty braids, ten on each side, before going to sleep, so the next morning my hair would be full and kinky and frizzy, like my glam-band boys in Poison and White Snake and Van Halen and Def Leppard. My mother scoffed. She said I looked like a lion.

By high school, the desire for a perm-like-the-other-girls dissipated. My hair was still long and straight and still its original color, making me an oddball among my female peers, and all those junior high perms had fizzled out into limp half-curls. With gift money in my pocket one Christmas break, I stopped at the mall, alone, and lingered outside a beauty salon. Within an hour I'd gotten my first real haircut— a professional shampoo, a conservative trim of only an inch or two, and bangs cut at an angle that officially took me away from the straight-across and *very* out of style look. It was the first time I'd washed my hair with something other than my mom's shampoo of choice, a heavy, creamy brand called Silkience. I was almost seventeen.

❀❀❀❀

Vines tougher than wrists
And rubbery shoots,
Scums, mildews, smuts along stems,
Great cannas or delicate cyclamen tips, –
. . . Fifty summers in motion at once,
As the live heat billows from pipes and pots.
    —Theodore Roethke

One of my favorite jobs at the greenhouse was one I invented, untangling the clematis vines. We sold the clematis in the spring and summer, in little square black pots that the young plants quickly outgrew. Each plant was allocated a short wooden stake on which, in practice, its eager vines could wrap themselves. They never obeyed, and within a week the adventurous vines were tangled around each other, the benches, even the frame of the greenhouse. During slow moments I would abandon my cash register position and untangle the wild lot of them, patiently unwrapping vine after vine, retraining them along their given stakes. I never cut a vine, never snapped one out of a complex tangle. Within days, longer and voracious, the vines were out of control again, wrapping around the sturdy stalk of neighboring perennials. I spent entire summers with the clematis, their great untangler.

❀❀❀❀

Where were the greenhouses going,
Lunging into the lashing
Wind driving water
So far down the river
  —Theodore Roethke

For thirty days after my outing to We Care Hair, I absolutely obsessed about whether or not my hair was too short. I avoided mirrors. At other times, I couldn't look enough. It was as if I was the first woman in the world to get a haircut, and I assumed everyone knew, and that everyone thought my choice was a bad idea, a shame.

I stalked through the mall just to stare at other women's hair, memorizing where it fell down their backs, judging mine against theirs. Although I liked how my hair felt without six inches of ragged, tangled split ends, I was unexpectedly distraught that I no longer had the longest hair. I never realized the strange little pleasure of wet hair down my back in the shower until that hair was gone.

Eventually, using a tape measure, I looked at how long a half inch was, because Jennifer-the-stylist estimated that my hair grew half an inch a month. I stretched the tape measure out to six inches, which, in theory, was how much my hair would grow back in a year. I held the tape measure at the end of my hair, pressing it against the flat of my back. I calmed down. I would have long hair again. And it would be healthy, smooth, shiny, unbroken, and I'd take good care of it this time and let it grow even longer—a future I subconsciously wished for my parents.

❦❦❦❦

The truth is the lie you once told returning to haunt you.
—Dermot Healy

My mother's reactions to my few haircuts were always loaded with suspicion. She often commented, "I see you got your hair cut," in the same tone of voice she reserved for "I see you came home late last night." I was left to linger on those seven words, reading between them, around them, through them. Did she approve? Was she annoyed? Why did it matter? I could never tell. In college, when for four years my hair routinely took on the vibrant shades of Manic Panic hair dye (first blue, then green, red, purple, or yellow, wonderful stuff without peroxide, and it washed out in a month), my mother refused to comment at all, a reaction I read as surrender. I partly wanted her to take the bait. If she uttered one word about my choice of color, I'd be quick with a critical comment about her bleached and blonded hair. I knew its real color was light brown, with hints of gray.

The weird thing is, when she had her sister cut her hair, I didn't even notice. I'd just arrived home for some holiday visit, and we'd hugged and bustled around the kitchen, when she asked "Do you like it?"

Like what? I thought, completely confused. She flipped her hand through her short hair. *My god.* I was not so much stunned by the shortness as I was by my absolute blindness. How did I miss such a momentous change? When I walked through the door, how could I have been unaware that for the first time in my existence my mom had short hair? Caught between a thousand reactions, I stared.

She smiled. "It was time for a change."

Later, she commented that she had recently fallen down when the wind blew her hair across her face, and she misstepped as she tried to brush it aside with her hands, which were semiparalyzed in half fists. I

Dad, me, and the pets, circa 1978

realized how many times a day I, without thinking, slid my hair behind
my ears, or effortlessly wrapped it behind me, out of the way.

I have never told her I cut so much off after the graduation weekend.
I hid in Iowa for nine months until most had grown back and the cutline
didn't look so severe. I did not want to acknowledge what that haircut
symbolized—my reaction against a deeply irrational fear that since my
father left my mother, and since I looked like my mother, he would
someday leave me, too.

❀❀❀❀

This flower is scorched
This film is on, on a maddening loop
These clothes don't fit us right
And I'm to blame
It's all the same, it's all the same
You come to me with a bone in your hand
You come to me with your hair curled tight
          —R.E.M.

My father's curly, wild brown hair is the feature that sets him apart from his parents and siblings, who all wore their hair cropped and neat. I once asked him why he wore it like that, and he said, "I want to look like Charles Manson," an unsettling and absurd comment meant to cause commotion for the sake of attention. It's partly an ongoing rebellion against something. I'm not precisely sure against what. He likes to tell the college story about applying for a driver's education job but getting denied because he refused to shave his moustache. He eventually complemented the moustache with a beard.

When my father shaved his beard and moustache in an attempt to "look credible" during the divorce proceedings, I could not look at him. I had driven home to Ohio for the holidays and had made the greenhouse my first stop. Despite being entrenched in splitting up, my parents were still working together, side-by-side in the main office. So as I greeted Mom in the office, she gave me a split-second warning, "Your father shaved his beard today." Then there he was, beardless, like half his face was gone. I looked away immediately, stared hard out the office window at all things familiar, the wild growth of tropical plants, the snow on a glass roof, and the leftover holiday arrangements. *I hardly recognized him.* He had a tiny chin, a sad chin, like a child's chin. It was pale, almost translucent. It was a terrible moment. I'd been closer to my dad than my mom, following him step by step through our labyrinth of greenhouses, eager to get my hands dirty in the same soil he expertly bedded around so many stems and roots. And now he was different, guilty, wrong.

"You look good," I lied.

It was easier than I imagined.

The Grotto of the Redemption

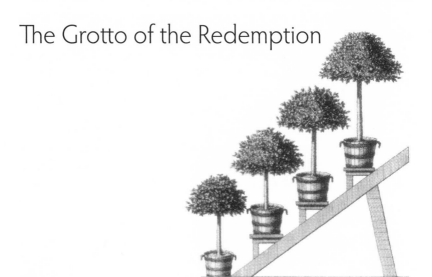

Kelly and I are twirling in the middle of the largest grotto in the world one day after Halloween in the year 2000. Kelly's short hair is purple, green, and white. She sports plastic Hello Kitty ears and a red corduroy dress over baggy jeans cut off mid-calf to reveal red and yellow striped socks. Her sleeveless dress shows off a dancing fairy tattoo circling her right bicep. My hair is long and dark blonde, tangled down the back of a purple velvet cape. I'm wearing a turquoise nurse's shirt, a gauzy rainbow skirt that was stylish in the 1990s, and black leather boots from Hamburg. The cape is from London. The shirt is from Goodwill. Kelly is from San Francisco. I am from Ohio. This is West Bend, Iowa. We are visiting the Grotto of the Redemption.

(O afflicted one, storm-tossed, and not comforted, behold)

The twirling is Kelly's idea. Her camera sits on a rocky ledge, catching us. Dizzy, we stumble around a corner and startle a middle-aged couple. They smile uneasily, but being polite Midwesterners, they wait for us to catch our breath and regain our balance. The woman glances at our outfits. The man tips his cap. It's a farmer's cap, green, with mesh across the back and "Agri-Pro" in gold stitching on the front. It's not so much *on* his head as it is *on top* of his head.

"Welcome to the Grotto," he says. "Where you girls from?"

"Ohio," I say.

"San Francisco," says Kelly.

"Well," says the man.

His wife folds creases into a brochure.

"Will you take our picture?" asks Kelly, handing him her camera.

The man nods. His wife crosses her arms, but smiles briefly. Kelly and I splay our bodies against the grotto walls in mock ecstasy, angling our hips, our breasts, our necks, cocking an eyebrow, parting our lips, caught in glorious, kitschy rapture.

(I will set your stones in antimony)

This one city block of West Bend, Iowa, contains four million dollars' worth of jewels, minerals, shiny rocks, and even Day-Glo plastic, all set in cement arches, caverns, walls and staircases. This creation is called the Grotto of the Redemption.

Father Paul Dobberstein vowed to create the Grotto in 1897, shortly after his appointment to the St. Peter and Paul Catholic Church in West Bend. Upon his arrival, he fell ill. His fever held at 101. His breath hung like wet sheets in his lungs. Parishioners fed him warm broth and wondered if he'd die before they even got to know him. Delusional with an onslaught of double pneumonia, Father Dobberstein prayed to the Virgin Mary to save him. If she did, he'd build her the most magnificent grotto.

He survived, and began the Grotto in 1912, with stalagmites cut from the floor of Jewel Cave in the Black Hills of South Dakota. He worked alone, from memory, from what he had beheld deep in his pneumonia fever. No one questioned him, and why would they? The inspired blend of jewels and icons thrilled the parishioners accustomed to traditional worship. This was rapture made real. Folks donated what they could: money, stones, cement, praise. They watched a magnificent, bizarre monument rise outside the church. Iowans and Catholics would come to call it the Eighth Wonder of the World.

For the next forty-two years, Father Dobberstein traveled the world, collecting rocks and jewels and hauling them to West Bend, a portion of the Midwest completely devoid of pretty minerals. Rubies, sapphires, fool's gold, lodestones, moonstones, onyx, amethysts and agates. Ocean coral. Badland slag. More stalagmites cut from the cave floors of the Ozarks and Carlsbad. Shards of glass he found in the street. He set them all in foundations of cement. Driven and guided by religious blueprints in his head, he clung to a verse from the book of Isaiah:

O afflicted one, storm-tossed, and not comforted, behold, I will set your stones in antimony, and lay your foundations with sapphires. I will make your pinnacles of agate, your gates of carbuncles, and all your walls of precious stones. All your sons shall be taught by the Lord, and great shall be the prosperity of your sons.

—Isaiah 54:11-13

His vision was to build a large grotto made up of smaller grottoes representing nine important religious moments. Father Dobberstein started with the Grotto of the Garden of Eden and wanted to end with the Grotto of the Resurrection. The goal was to show the beauty and power of Christ's redemption through the beauty and power of precious stones set in caverns of cement. These minerals and jewels, famed for their durability, would symbolize the strength of the church. They would dazzle and awe the common believers. The glint of jewels would spark reverence and devotion.

(and lay your foundations with sapphires)

From the parking lot, the Grotto resembles a half-finished castle because it has no roof. There are at least five white statues of angels, arms uplifted, bugles to lips, wings tilted in perpetual take-off, pious guardians on the walls. From this distance, the walls appear mostly brown and white. Kelly and I don't know that in a few minutes we'll see interior walls studded with carefully planned patterns of all colors. A tall plain church is behind the Grotto. Modest houses are on the left and right. Kelly can sense something special. From the parking lot to the front wall, a distance of about a hundred yards, she takes twelve photos and announces *"I cannot fucking believe this!"* at least six times.

We enter under a jeweled arch straight out of a fantasy world. The Grotto spreads into a series of caves, passages, stairs, balconies, and towers. Kelly and I are swept into complete silence for a few minutes as we orient ourselves to this unusual circumstance of being surrounded by four million dollars worth of jewels. All we can say is *wow*. We walk side by side, like little girls, into the first small cave on our right. It is cool, shadowed, a secret sphere of condensation. A plaque tells us it is "The Garden of Eden Grotto (Paradise Lost)." There's a real emerald snake laced through real emerald leaves of the infamous Tree of Knowledge, a tree set in stone in the wall.

Up close, the magnitude of jewels in the Grotto walls gives me the feeling that Father Dobberstein kept revising his plans as he worked, evidenced by the Garden of Eden Grotto's domed ceiling above the snake-and-tree mosaic. It arches twenty feet, covered in a pattern of split geodes. The geodes, rocks that when split in half reveal cavities of crystals, would have been enough. Their sparkling centers suggest a beauty of creation beyond human perceptions. And that there are about one hundred set in cement above me is dazzling. Spotlights from the floor shine up, catching the sparkle. I look closer. In the center of each geode stands an upright piece of petrified wood, like an altar, and at the tip of each altar is a tiny fragment of pink rock I can't identify. Father Dobberstein must have glued the pink fragments to the wood, and the wood to the geodes. I realize the geodes are mini-grottoes within the Garden of Eden Grotto within the Grotto of the Redemption. I realize Father Dobberstein was a truly inspired man.

Between the geodes are swirls of pink and white quartz. I can't see the cement foundation. Every inch has been set with something. Framing the Eden entrance are hundreds of long spiral seashells. From inside the Eden Grotto looking out, I notice the spiral shells frame a walkway of fifteen-foot tall spires that lead deeper in the Grotto, and the walkway ends with a view of the church's steeple. The natural shell spirals, the distant spires in their frame, and the geodesic grottoes in the Eden

Grotto are a complex creativity, one only Father Dobberstein understood. Kelly and I catch each other wide-eyed more than once. There
is simply so much to see.

All nine of the little grottoes are like this, complex in structure and
layered with religious meaning. Neither Kelly nor I have religion. We
have little respect and less knowledge. Kelly rebelled early on against
her Lutheran upbringing. She was a new student in my public junior
high school when she was thirteen, when her young mom remarried,
and Kelly left her Lutheran school. My family, all the way back to my
grandparents, mostly ignored religion and church. In elementary school,
I had some friends whose families were devout. I felt sorry for them.
They had to attend church early on Sunday mornings, and they had to
feel guilty all the time because, to hear their mothers put it, God was
cataloguing their many sins at all moments of the day. I once asked my
parents what religion we were, and they told me we had the religion of
nature, whatever that meant. I was baptized in the United Church of
Christ, then never attended. In my teen years I refused to be confirmed.
I was very keen about hypocrisy. I hadn't been to church in a decade and
now my mom wanted me to be confirmed? I would have none of it.

In college, I took a class on the history of the New Testament. Then
I took a class on the history of Eastern religion. I reveled in the aca-
demic approach. At the same time, my boyfriend was a Jehovah's Witness.
To keep his parents at bay, I studied with his congregation every few
weeks. This was much to the annoyance of my parents, who were convinced I was on the verge of abandoning a pricey liberal arts education
to distribute the *Watchtower* three days a week.

My religious background is eclectic, my view of organized religion
skeptical, but I become a Grotto believer in a matter of minutes.

Kelly and I don't know the Stations of the Cross or the story of
Gethsemane. We don't know how to pronounce *Gethsemane*. We don't
even know all the Ten Commandments for sure. We walk through each
little grotto, patiently reading various biblical versus set in stone, trying
to assimilate the symbolism and the doctrine. Neither of us knows
enough about Catholicism to make definitive sense of any of it. But that
doesn't matter. Kelly and I are profoundly impressed, not because we

feel the call of Catholicism, but because we are both creative people. Kelly sews her own wild clothes, can work wonders with tattered Goodwill rejects, and dreams up hair styles and hair colors I've never seen duplicated. I write stories and essays and poems. We respect Father Dobberstein's vision.

We're not supposed to touch anything. Warning signs every ten feet remind us. We give the signs due consideration and then cup our hands into the geodes and press our cheeks against emeralds. We pat the toes of a Jesus statue. I take Kelly's picture, one of the ninety pictures we'll end up with, as she pretends to drink from a chalice held by an angel. We touch as many splendid stones as possible. Beauty is more real when touched.

(I will make your pinnacles of agate)

Father Dobberstein died before the Grotto was completely finished, or so the myth of the man goes. The brochure plays up his 1897 near-death event with the Virgin Mary, but details of his final breath are scant. The death of such a man is complicated, full of theological pitfalls. For if he was near death once, and the Virgin Mary saved him, reason suggests he would pray to her again when death came near a second time. And during this vision, he would not just *promise* to build her a grotto; he'd have the evidence on hand. He'd be able to say, "Look! Look what I've been building for you! Let me live so I can continue." And if she didn't let him live?

I don't think he ever planned on finishing it. That was the catch. I think Father Dobberstein believed he'd found immortality within the Grotto, within the everlasting composition of minerals and jewels and the timeless tales of Christ. According to his vision, the Virgin Mary herself had approved the Grotto. Father Dobberstein had to redeem himself in her eyes. He needed to stay alive in order to accomplish this task. And if the Grotto was never in a final stage of completion, Father Dobberstein would need to live a little bit longer so he could reach that stage. Maybe Father Dobberstein's biggest secret was his belief that he was a chosen immortal, that he was, in essence, strong as gold, privileged as diamonds, glorious as alabaster.

A succession of deacons puzzled over the structure until 1994, completing what they could, based on what few writings Father Dobberstein left behind. When they couldn't quite figure out what else Father Dobberstein had planned, they built a gift shop and a mineral shop and a restaurant and a duck pond. They installed flood lights and a sound system.

They commissioned a life-sized bronze statue of Father Dobberstein, which they set on a pile of white rocks. When Kelly and I find the statue behind the Grotto, we're amused. The Father doesn't look the part. The statue has him wearing a baseball cap and a cardigan, slacks and casual shoes. His left arm is outstretched like he's just tossed a horseshoe. In his right, a rock hammer swings. He has an "aw-shucks" grin on his face. He's not looking at his beloved grotto, but towards the back end of the church.

Tours start every hour on the hour, May to October. There has never been an entrance fee, only a small donation box. One-hundred thousand people visit a year. Six million have visited since 1912. The day after Halloween, in the year 2000, Kel and I are two of four total visitors.

(your gates of carbuncles)

Moments after critiquing the statue, when we think nothing will ever top the Grotto, we spot the Grotto Gift Shop. Kelly, accustomed to her raucous San Francisco lifestyle, howls with glee from all corners of the store, flashing her tri-color hair and filling a shopping basket with trinkets. Inured to the manners of the Midwest, I browse silently through postcards, admiring aerial shots. The quiet, gray-haired clerk sits behind the counter, then stands, then sits. Then she folds some tissue paper. I smile at the postcards.

Our big find is a framed watercolor of a mullet-haired Jesus playing volleyball with white kids. Kelly is a connoisseur of kitschy Americana, and she nearly weeps. She's so pleased. She wants to buy one or two of everything. The Volleyball Jesus tempts her, as do wooden Grotto coasters and "official Grotto crystals" strung on gold chains. She settles on purchasing a plastic Virgin Mary hot-glued to a shiny stone, with a misproportioned fake carnation towering over her. She considers it one of the greater acquisitions of her life. Kelly implores me to purchase what she says is a rare, black-skinned, plastic Virgin Mary lawn ornament. I almost buy it, this fantastic example of the white world's awkward, absurd attempt at racial integration. But in a fleeting moment of seriousness I realize that such a thing honestly isn't for me, and that there's something wrong with buying a black Virgin Mary for sheer ironic value. Instead, I fall back on what's practical: eighteen books of Grotto matches, a deck of Grotto cards in a plastic case, and a laminated Grotto bookmark with a pretty blue ribbon. The bookmark has a picture of Father Dobberstein with his hands on the heads of two St. Bernard dogs.

The clerk carefully wraps our purchases in tissue paper and compliments our outfits as "cute Halloween costumes." She adjusts her gold-rimmed glasses and beams with warmth and pride when Kelly tells her the Grotto of the Redemption is the coolest thing she's ever seen.

(and all your walls of precious stones.)

The Grotto of the Redemption is an anomaly among grottoes because it is so big, so public, and it exceeds the classic grotto requirements. The first natural grottoes were shallow caves among the foothills of mountains in Europe. They weren't ornamented. Shepherds would spend nights in the caves, lighting candles, hanging religious adornments, whispering prayers. The caverns became places of protection and worship, like hidden churches, and so *grotto* took on the connotation of *secret* and *powerful*. They were strange, curious places, even grotesque. Shepherds returning to their villages praised the grottoes as places of deep religious influence, and so the villagers soon created easily accessible grottoes. The intown grottoes were small, cozy, intended for one person, not designed to replace the churchgoing experience but to enhance it. Today, only a few people visit the Grotto out of religious need. Others come out of curiosity. Some make it a stop between the Field of Dreams in Dyersville, Iowa, and the Corn Palace in Sioux City. People live across the street from it.

As I tour the grotto in West Bend, I find myself thinking about the name. Historically, all grottoes were grottoes of redemption. That was their point. I want to line edit the name of this place. Most of all, I want to leave out the second *the* in its name—The Grotto of Redemption, not The Grotto of *The* Redemption, and I want to lowercase those letters. I want to make it private, secular, and small again.

Kelly and I have been pulled to the Grotto out of disbelief that something so grand, so idolatrous, so unusual, exists in Iowa. If there is anything blatantly unredeemed in our lives, we're quiet about it, for the most part. We have no grand awakenings at the Grotto. No religious experiences. No visions. No need for *The Redemption*, but maybe we have the need for redemption.

I have been living in Ames, Iowa, for almost three years, first for grad school at Iowa State University, then for a job as a reading teacher. Kelly, my high school marching band drumline cohort, is visiting on her way back home to Ohio. She has lived in San Francisco for four years, but her stepfather died last spring. He had cancer. He was young, the cancer swift. He and Kelly hadn't always been on good terms. Then Kelly's longtime girlfriend dumped her for a butch bartender. Kelly quit her job at a Planned Parenthood in a ghetto mall near Oakland. She told me she'd seen too many fights in the waiting room. She packed up her little black Honda with everything she owned and headed east, to be with her widowed mother and her sixteen-year-old stepbrother.

Iowa is the halfway mark on her trip. She already has a new job at a Planned Parenthood in a posh suburb outside Cleveland. She's excited that her future patients will know how to read and take birth control pills and not eat tree bark when they crave minerals while pregnant. Her sarcasm is wonderful and we laugh all day, but I know how uneasy she is about returning to Ohio. It was the place we wanted to get away from, and in my eyes, Kelly succeeded with style. She made it all the way to San Francisco. She's returning to be with the family she once couldn't wait to get away from. She can't explain it, just asserts that it's the right thing to do, and the most difficult thing to do. She's scared she won't make any new friends back in Ohio, like she's still that shy thirteen-year-old at a new junior high.

Our conversation makes me consider the right thing to do. I confess to her my own problems. When I learned my parents were divorcing,

Snow on the roof of a plastic hoop house, December 2003

that my mother's MS was worsening, I panicked over the possibility that I would have to return to Ohio to take care of my mother. I didn't want to do it. It would not be fair. I wasn't the sick one; I wasn't the one in a disastrous marriage. What wasn't my fault wasn't my responsibility. Kelly says she understands, which means that she understands me, my ego, my self-centeredness, and my anger.

We worry, together, curiously, what our absences have done and will do to our families.

(All your sons shall be taught by the Lord,)

Before we leave the Grotto, we sit in a sunny spot near the north wall because that's where David Lynch filmed part of his movie *The Straight Story*. It's a true story about Alvin Straight, an old Iowan who rode his lawnmower from Iowa to Wisconsin so he could make amends with his sick older brother. He had to ride the mower because he couldn't see well enough to drive a car legally. He refused to ask his daughter, played by Sissy Spacek, for any help. He was an archetypal Iowan, elderly, driven by the need to do right, pestered by a long-ago error, self-sufficient to a fault. Richard Farnsworth played Alvin. Farnsworth looked like Einstein would have had he been a farmer. Lynch filmed Farnsworth riding the lawnmower past the Grotto in a scene that lasted about five seconds. When I saw *The Straight Story* in a theater in Des Moines, the audience clapped when they saw old Alvin at the Grotto. The entire movie was filmed on locations in Iowa and Wisconsin, but only the Grotto earned mid-movie applause.

I would have done most anything to ask David Lynch, the surreal cinematic mind behind *Twin Peaks* and *Eraserhead,* what he thought about the Grotto. It's a good enough substitute to lean against a wall he probably looked at.

Kelly takes more pictures and I consider a brochure the clerk has slipped into my bag. Along with all the Grotto facts and history, the brochure tells me the countryside around West Bend is filled with "wise and prosperous farmers." I tell Kelly and we snicker over this threefold half truth. The numbers of farmers and their prosperity has changed so radically since the brochure was printed, and the label of "wise" makes me think only of the three wise men.

I take out a book of matches and remove the cracked cellophane wrapping. The book is like a double book. It holds forty matches, not twenty. It's rectangular so pictures of the Grotto can fit on the front and back. Inside, there's an advertisement for the West Bend Motel. "One block north of the Grotto, eighteen modern units, TV and Air Conditioning, Reasonable Rates. Dial 3611." Behind the matches is a map of Iowa with a big blue star over West Bend. The match tips appear to be covered in mold.

"What the hell," I say. "These are a hundred years old."

I twist off a match and strike it. Nothing. I try again and the tip sizzles to flame. It smells funny, like I imagine mold on fire would smell. The flame slips back into the tip in two seconds. The tendril of smoke is noxious.

"Do you know," says Kelly, "how many of my San Francisco friends would kill to get high here?" I nod. I'm already making a mental list of friends who ought to visit the Grotto, hopped up or utterly sober.

I light another match. The mold intrigues me. I ask Kelly if it's safe to use matches with mold on them. I think she ought to know the answer. She has no idea.

We sit for a very long time. It's November, warm. Brown leaves catch in the strange corners of the Grotto. Other than the polite couple and the gift shop clerk, we have not seen any other visitors. Even the houses across the street look empty. The Grotto is ours. I fiddle with my camera. Outside the Grotto earlier, I noticed it didn't work. But inside, it's fine. I smack the battery case with the heel of my hand. I don't want my camera to be religious like this.

Later I'll learn that locals swear tornadoes bear down on the Grotto but never damage it. It sits exposed year-round, without a security fence or alarm system to guard the jewels, without a roof to thwart the Midwestern blizzards, without shade trees to cool the hundred-degree summer heat. The foundations are not cracked. It was threatened, but not seriously, by the floods of 1993, when most of Iowa was under at least a couple feet of Mississippi water for an entire summer. No one drops trash in the little grottoes, and no one picks at loose gems along the walls. Maybe the gems never loosen. In its ninety years of existence, the Grotto has never been seriously marred.

I cannot help but compare it to my greenhouses shimmering in the sun of another Midwest. Encase the greenhouse glass in cement, or reset jewels in thin frames of wood, and the grotto and the greenhouse doppelgang each other. The Grotto is actually many grottoes; the greenhouse, many greenhouses. Yet visitors speak of them by their singular versions. "The Grotto." "The Greenhouse." Many people came to our greenhouse just to walk through, to look at all the plants. Like the Grotto, it could be a place for meandering, for contemplation. The

The South House at night, 1943. Reprinted with permission from Florists' Review Enterprises

Grotto of the Redemption is full of strange twists and nooks, none visible from the outside. So too our greenhouse. From outside, the greenhouse is all rectangular geometry. But from inside, the curve of plant leaves softens the grid of glass. Their green mosaics tell the stories I know. It's the eighth wonder of my world.

I want to believe that Sam Hirt built the greenhouse from a vision, and I want to believe that all visions hold the same merit, be they fleeting or life-consuming, secular or divine. Why? Why does a structure become more important when it is born from a vision? I do not know, but I see the effects. The Grotto will always be protected and preserved, like a cathedral. Part of me wishes that the greenhouse could have that same status, earning automatic respect. Or maybe I just wish I could hand out brochures about it.

The Jehovah's Witness boyfriend once told me that whenever he drove by the greenhouse, he couldn't help but hold it in high reverence, to look

with awe and respect upon the structure. His own congregation, fierce-
ly critical of idols, met three times a week in a windowless, round room
with artificial lighting and sturdy carpet. There was a podium and a
microphone in place of an altar or natural acoustics. He admitted to his
fascination with the huge glass structure as if he were confessing. Years
after we split, I offered via email to give him a piece of glass from the
greenhouse, before it was demolished. He responded with rapid enthusiasm. I could imagine him accepting the relic with hands cupped.

One reason my family never went to church is because we always
worked on Sundays, taking advantage of the post-church crowd. I knew
the holidays not by the corresponding biblical stories, but by the corresponding plants. Poinsettias and cyclamen at Christmas, hyacinths
and lilies at Easter. As a kid, I could identify the leaves of Jacob's Ladder,
the blooms of the passionflower, or the spikes of the Crown of Thorns
succulents. I knew their prices and care requirements. But I would have
been dumbstruck if someone opened a Bible and read me the relevant
passages.

On our way out of town, Kelly and I search in vain for the West Bend
Motel, the vague directions on the matchbook proving to be from an
epoch long past. We stop at a Dairy Queen for dinner and wait ten minutes
for fried fish sandwiches. Iowa loves Dairy Queens. There is at least one
per town, sometimes two, no Baskin Robbins and their thirty-one flavors
in sight. I once asked a Dairy Queen employee why they only offered
vanilla and chocolate. "Because of all the toppings," he told me.

Kelly says she wishes she had bought the black Virgin Mary lawn
ornament. I give her some moldy matches and we agree to exchange
doubles of our photos. We finish our fish sandwiches, which are deli-
cious, and share an Oreo Blizzard on the drive back to Ames. I talk,
complain, for endless Iowan miles about my father and his immoral
affairs, until Kelly says sharply, over the red straw in the Blizzard, "At
least he's still alive."

I'm thrown into introspection by the barbs of her comment, remem-
bering Father Dobberstein's bargain with his fever vision of Mary. In
graduate school I learned why some people say that all art is about death.

We create art so that we will be remembered after we've died. Art is a piece of us left behind for contemplation. If the quintessential human fear is being forgotten, and if the reaction to that fear is to create, then Father Dobberstein must have been disquieted with dread. I think I know how he feels.

(and great shall be the prosperity of your sons.)

Kelly leaves my apartment the next morning. We hug and she gives me a cutting from her jade plant. The jade is her favorite, riding across the country in her passenger seat. She's had it since she was an angry lesbian college student in Missoula. The jade's stem will need to sit in water for a few months until roots sprout. The only jelly jar I have is too tall, so I fashion a tiny brace out of twist-ties. I secure the brace below the bottom leaves. This way, I can set the cutting in the water and let the ends of the twist-ties catch the edge of the jar, keeping the leaves above water. I place it on the windowsill over the kitchen sink.

It stays in that jar for ten months, growing wispy wet roots, until I drive it back west, not to California but to Idaho. Daily, I wonder how content it is with just water, this water baby, how it curves toward the light with such diligence that sometimes, by evening, it has toppled out of the jar in a devoted feat of movement, so hungry for the sun it fore-goes the sanctity of water.

(Isaiah 54:11-13)

Best Offer

In June of 2001, I needed to sell my car, a jade 1998 Honda CRV with 47,000 miles on the odometer. The reasons were multiple but simple. First, I had quit my job as a reading tutor in favor of three more years of graduate school in Idaho. The decision involved a significant pay cut. Second, my parents, who had helped with the monthly car payments, were rerouting all their money into a lengthy divorce. Their three decades of wedded bliss were over, and so was their history of joint ownership of twelve cars—two for me, two for my brother, and eight for them. A year out of graduate school, with all my peers hot for jobs and trying to buy cars, not sell them, I was doing the opposite. At a time when twenty-somethings like me were all well adjusted to their broken families, I was just learning how to traverse the domestic rifts. It seemed like keeping the car would be a fast way to accelerate headfirst into one of those rifts. There was the practical financial rift of no longer having an income for the $383 monthly car payments, which would drain my savings by Independence Day. There was the complicated emotional rift of no longer wanting the gift car, a heady symbol of what my once-married parents had been eager to bestow.

So on a humid afternoon I angled into the only open parking spot of South Main Used Car Sales in Ames, Iowa. The lot was modest, urban, crowded. It was operated by Honda, which had a full-size car lot and showroom just down the street.

Used cars were lined up three deep. Clearly, my Honda CRV was the newest kid in the lot, a youngster held in distrust by the tired minivans and rusted sedans, their trends long past. I sat still for a full minute, nervous, like the day I had to take my driving test through the tricky one-way streets of Medina, Ohio. I had never dealt with a used car salesman. I didn't know the customs of this trade. The lot could have been a foreign nation. I didn't have a guidebook or a companion who spoke the language. I considered the embarrassment of being swindled.

For my entire life I had seen people cling to their cars, through oil crises and recession, through bankruptcy and defaults, accidents, suspensions, fatalities. Cars seemed to define so many people. As long as they had their cars, they were okay. But cars limit, too, and I was ready to admit the limitations of my car.

My Honda CRV was a "small" compact sports utility vehicle. Like a trendy station wagon on a truck frame. It was not as goofy-looking as its immediate competitor, Toyota's RAV4, and it was more reliable than the KIA Sportage. It was not so, shall we politely say, *large* as a traditional SUV. Not the Ford Excursion, which is nineteen feet long and does not fit well into garages or parking spaces. Not an Expedition, not a Suburban, not a Mountaineer or a Hummer.

In late 1997, Honda marketed the brand new CRV to my demographic, the young educated female, single, maybe childless and career-oriented, probably with a decent job in the suburbs or a small city, ready for the occasional jaunt to a campground. In other words, someone who was a DINK–Double Income, No Kids. My boyfriend and I laughed at ourselves when we learned the DINK definition. We met the requirements with near perfection. Along with the double income part, DINKs tended to put off marriage, earn graduate degrees, and own expensive pets. We had three sable ferrets, and our graduate degrees and our lack of wedding pictures. Being pegged as DINKs was somehow better than yuppies, but not much. We had to concede. We couldn't see any way out of it. The fact that I drove a Honda CRV capped it off, and I felt more than a little unsettled.

I did not grasp the true meaning of *unsettled* until my parents pursued their divorce, which proved to be a stunning financial drain on a family used to a big house, country acreage with horses and a barn, computers and televisions for everyone, loan-free college educations, and cars, cars, and more cars.

The CRV had been a going-to-grad-school present. At the time, I had a blue Chevy Beretta, but at the news of my plans to move from Ohio to Iowa, the car retaliated. Wires frizzled in the engine, causing the car to stall, first only in rain and then whenever it felt like it. Then there was a flat tire, and rust spots damaged the hood after a harsh winter. The car was seven years old, and it was not nearly as eager as I for the seven-hundred-mile drive from Ohio to Iowa. My parents were worried. Then they offered the new CRV. "For Iowa."

I expected the offer but was somewhat suspicious. Did they really have the money for this? On the other hand, I was certainly not going to turn down a chance for someone to buy me a twenty-thousand-dollar car. Dad explained that they would use my brother's college money. My brother, two years younger and "having a hard time maturing," had dropped out of college, twice.

Because my parents had always executed financial maneuvers with nonchalance, and because my winning streak in the stacked contest of sibling rivalry had been complete and absolute for a long time, the monetary details were not a big deal to me. The big deal shifted to the quirks of the car, like its picnic table. How absurd, a car outfitted with a table, of all things. The back floor of the cargo area could be removed, plastic legs unfolded, and you had yourself a table. The brochures hyped it as a picnic table, but it was more like a novelty card table. Everyone raved about the picnic table. I never used it.

Two years after I drove that shiny car right off the lot, a fat envelope arrived in the mail. From Mom, it was full of payment coupons for a car loan. It was barely halfway paid off. I was stunned. Why hadn't they used my brother's college money? Was that a joke I missed?

The payments were $383 a month, and with three years left on the contract, I was suddenly in debt for over $13,700. I felt like I'd been had. Tricked. Slapped down for my privileged assumptions. My parents had made it easy to feel entitled, and the reverse stopped me sharp. Struggling with their divorce, they had done more than toss me from the nest. They had tossed me from the garage. I wanted to complain, but with whispers of "spoiled" haunting my conscience, I didn't. I was stuck.

Every American teen goes through an initiation into the family garage. They're either given a car or the keys to a car with a million strings attached but it doesn't matter. The teen is finally on the threshold of one undeniable tenet of American life, driving anywhere, at any cost, coast to coast or border to border, using all the main streets in between.

My initiation was royal. My parents' manic excitement on the afternoon they brought home my first car made me wonder if they had conceived me with that moment in mind. For a week before my sixteenth birthday in February 1991, they had been applauding the virtues of a 1991 Chevy Beretta, blue, two doors, cassette deck and radio, air bags, power steering, anti-lock brakes. It was safe. It was new. It was perfect for a teenager. I was about to attain a level of independence otherwise unknown in my rural Ohio life. I was on my way to at least 200,000 miles of driving, to maybe 10,000 gallons of gas costing $12,000, to flat tires and snow storms, speeding tickets and near accidents, two summers of pizza delivery, and more freedom, more glorious freedom, than I could ever imagine.

I have often considered exactly why my parents bought the Beretta. They just paid for the whole thing and handed me the keys and there I was, the only teen in my class, maybe in my entire high school, with a new car. The first reasons for this bestowal of wheels were practical. My parent's cars were sport cars, stick shifts. Mom drove a sleek Dodge

Stealth, Dad a shocking red Toyota MR2, with its engine in back instead of under the hood. Insurance to cover me driving those cars would have been outlandish.

The other reasons were more abstract, more convoluted and difficult. My baby-boomer parents grew up in fairly well off families, but they never quite had everything they wanted. They spoke bitterly of how their parents would only give to each child what they could give to all their children. It was an effort to dispel sibling rivalry. (It failed.) Mom and her three younger siblings did not get new cars; Dad and his two older siblings did not get new cars. They didn't get cars at all in 1963, when they were sixteen. They built grudges and constructed unhappy childhoods. By giving me a car, my parents were seeking reparations. I tried not to think about it too much. I appreciated the Beretta unconditionally, and the freedom it gave me largely defined who I was able to become in my final years of high school and throughout college.

Standing in the used car lot with my Honda CRV, fortifying my nerve so I could do what I was about to do, I decided to check out used cars for the first time in my life, just out of curiosity. All had mileages over eighty thousand. There were no other SUVs, compact or full-sized or behemoth, which made sense. America loved her large automobiles. Not wanting one was anti-family, anti-capitalist, maybe even communist.

I had read the anti-SUV articles. One was about a car co-op on the West Coast, where tenants in an apartment decided to pool their money and buy one car for the apartment, and they'd take turns using it. I was pleasantly surprised. What a good idea. Another one in *Harper's*, "Bad Sports: How We Learned to Stop Worrying and Love the SUV," by Paul Roberts, smacked me upside the head because it laid out the startling facts about America's car cult.

Roberts reported on his day at the Ford Dealership and his test drive of a Ford Excursion, at the time the "largest passenger vehicle on the planet." He wrote about the slick salesman pitching the thing as a "needs-based" car, for a mere forty thousand dollars. On the test drive around town, Roberts noticed the Excursion was averaging four miles to the gallon. There were other disturbing facts. The year before, Americans purchased almost six million SUVs, despite their appalling gas mileage and their propensity for rollovers. He covered the psychological aspect, too. First, there was the propaganda effect. SUVs gained support immediately after the Gulf War, because so many people had watched Humvees hunt down Saddam. Then there was this: as Americans grappled more and more with complex feelings of despair and hopelessness, someone in automobile marketing latched on to the idea of promoting a car as *capable*. Family cars were waning, and long gone were muscle cars. Capable car, capable person. It didn't matter, the marketers quickly realized, whether or not the buyer *needed* off-road capabilities. The buyer wanted to buy the *potential* for any situation. Roberts reported that 89 percent of SUV owners never drove off road. I was one of them.

Capability. I ended up with a Honda CRV for that reason alone. After grad school in Iowa, I secured a good job as a reading teacher, content to work for a year while my boyfriend completed his degree. But with my parent's divorce, the surprise car payments, I realized something. I wasn't emotionally capable of owning this car, even though my salary, my lifestyle, and all the advertisements and family precedent that tapped into my psyche told me I was.

I paid for the Honda for a year, from 2000 to 2001. I had never set aside that much money, each month, just for a car. My wage was fifteen dollars an hour full time, which made me downright wealthy compared to the salary I'd drawn as a grad student, but the irony of the vicious financial loop ate at me. I needed a car to get to work forty miles away, but I was obligated to work to pay for the car, which was costing me more than four hundred dollars a month. I called the financing bank and tried to negotiate lower payments. No luck. My parents had never paid more than the minimum payment each month, had even been late a few times. Reality rolled into view, like rows of nines on an odometer.

Gas prices topped off at $1.80 a gallon for the cheap stuff, the highest in all my years of driving. Twenty-five dollars filled the tank, and the fuel lasted a few days. Insurance rates caught me by surprise. My parents had always paid the insurance on the Beretta, and while I knew about insurance, I was appallingly naïve about premiums, deductibles, all of it. Then, a ball bearing disintegrated, a two-hundred-dollar, weeklong repair. Central Iowa hosted the worst winter in years, and every night I saw accidents along the icy interstates. Big SUVs toppled in ditches, smashed against compact cars near the median, skidding in front of trucks. That's when I looked at my Honda CRV, really look at it for what it was, and I thought, *expensive. That is all you are. You are an expense.*

Most of the cars in the used car lot were at least a decade old. Some of the minivans were more recent. There were six dirty pastel minivans and they filled the spots facing the traffic. Their windows sported over-sized neon price tags and words like "WOW" and "BARGAIN" framed in starburst explosions of marketing excitement. Two mechanics on the far side of the lot watched me.

I entered the small office. There were cubicles. One was empty. In the other, two men were signing papers and shaking hands. A simulated wood grain nameplate on the dividing wall identified Roy Smith as the Used Car Manager. I sat in the empty cubicle, jingling my keys so someone, perhaps Roy, knew I was waiting.

Roy and his customer emerged from the cubicle. Roy was outfitted in a casual, solid white get-up, as if he moonlighted as a cabana boy. The customer wore faded, thin jeans and a bland windbreaker. They approached a gray Volvo parked next to my Honda. Roy started explaining the Volvo's features to the customer, who was jittery and malnourished. The Volvo Man's cheeks were sunken. He chainsmoked and adjusted his sunglasses and answered his cell phone, all while nodding in Roy's direction at the appropriate times. He motioned to the luggage rack and Roy flagged a mechanic who removed it. I wondered why he needed a Volvo. Maybe he had kids, maybe he needed cargo space. But why remove the luggage rack? A Volvo was not a very sporty car with or without it. Every Volvo I'd ever seen had been gray. And if it wasn't gray, it wanted to be gray.

I was hooked, absorbing the interplay of Roy and the Volvo Man, until Roy waved off the buyer, who merged his new used car into the traffic, a malnourished minnow in the belly of a whale. My turn. With minimal words, we exchanged hellos and got down to business. First, Roy peered up into the wheel wells. Apparently, this was where to look when buying a used car, which confused me because I was thinking he'd check the engine first. He immediately found the two dents. One was on the plastic molding above the back right tire, from when I misjudged the distance to the garage wall. A surface dent. It happened years ago. Roy didn't think the metal was dented. He was right. I'd checked.

The other dent, on the front right side, was less than an hour old. On my way to the used car lot, near a construction site, a backhoe tearing asphalt catapulted a hefty chunk of debris. I was stopped at a light. I saw the chunk hurtling toward my car and had the solid understanding that it would hit my car, cause damage, and there was nothing I could do. It thunked and I swore.

Roy kept looking at the wheels, two, three times around. He examined the engine for a total of six seconds. I was curious about what Roy was seeing. I wanted him to talk to me the way he'd spoken with the Volvo Man.

I made an offhand comment about the car needing a wash.

Roy responded, "I see through all the dirt." His tone was flat as metal.

He noted the mileage. I was disappointed when he didn't compliment me on the low forty-seven thousand miles, the overall good condition of the car. I took appropriate care—an oil change every three thousand miles, the expensive maintenance at fifteen thousand and thirty thousand. I even scraped bugs off the headlights. My CRV had a garage in the winter. I kept the interior spotless, always vacuumed. No smoking permitted. I fastidiously picked up straw wrappers and french fry remnants. I stored the owner's manual in its original plastic bag, plus the maintenance book was filled out, and I had receipts in chronological order for everything from oil changes to tire rotations.

Roy dismissed all this. He asked, "Are you interested in buying a different car?"

I was not. I waited, mindful of Roy's packed car lot.

Roy looked at my knees. "Why do you want to sell your car?" He was, perhaps, wondering why I wasn't trying to sell it on my own.

I looked at Roy's knees, his clean white pants. That was, indeed, the question of the hour. Why the hell was I selling this very nice automobile my parents so wanted me to have? I had already paid a lot for it, an amount dwarfed only by the generous money my parents had also paid. Why not hang on and get it all paid off? I had not even mentioned my plans to my parents. I was drafting the explanatory email in my head, not to be sent until after the car was sold. The plan, regarding my parents, was to weigh costs and benefits, compare use now to projected use over the next few years, make a case for the environment, explain oil guilt and the jeopardy of the Arctic National Wildlife Refuge, point out hefty gas prices, and finally, elaborate on my growing distrust of "the American way of life," this destructive car culture, the false premise that every person needed a car, a big car, regardless of long-term costs.

The plan was not to invoke the divorce. Not to point out that they had said they would pay for the entire car. Not to rationalize that if I had known the payments would fall on me, I sure as hell would not have chosen such an expensive car. Nor was I going to let Roy know that I had no idea how to sell a car that I didn't fully own, given that I owed the financing bank so much money. I wasn't sure how to transfer the title and tags, how to make sure some stranger's check was valid.

I told Roy that for the next three years I'd be back in grad school, teaching part time and living ten minutes from campus. I owned a great bike, sturdy and reliable. And my boyfriend leased a car for a mere one hundred dollars a month, which we'd share.

If Roy had a reaction, I didn't know what it was. He continued to stare at my knees. Stoic. As was I. Like a standoff. There was so much Roy did not need to know about me. He was not my counselor. He was a used car salesman. Did he think anyone ever told him the total truth? Did he really think he could see through all the dirt?

Roy flipped through a booklet he had pulled from his back pocket. He nodded toward the car. "It's a 1999 CRV?"

"1998."

"List price is thirteen thousand dollars."

"So you'll buy it for that much?" I was floored. That was a lot of money. Enough.

"Long as there are no major engine problems."

We talked a bit about how the thirteen thousand dollars would be more than enough to cover the remainder of the loan, which was around nine thousand dollars. The amount left over would be all mine. Roy gave me some basic advice on contacting the bank and clearing the loan payoff through the Honda dealership. He offered his business card, white and crisp like his cabana-boy slacks. I realized that if I knew a damned thing about cars, I'd probably try to haggle him up for a better offer. I realized I didn't care. Roy caught my urgency and apprehension and he did an incredibly kind thing. He suggested I think about it for a few days. I said I would.

Because I never imbued my car with human characteristics, I didn't think my car was wondering what the hell we were doing at a used car lot that afternoon. I didn't worry that my car's stomach was knotting in anxiety. I didn't listen to my car cry and promise to do better tomorrow, if only I would not sell it. I didn't think it was getting lippy with me, demanding a definition of "used," because dammit, it still felt very new, if I wanted its opinion. I was not fretting about the next owner who might shove empty beer cans under the seats, play loathsome music, run a stop sign, cause accidents. I looked at my car's shiny headlights and thought, *expensive. You are an expensive piece of metal. That's all you are.*

I drove the car home, not listening to it make me feel bad for what I was about to do. *And all this time I've never broken down, not even when the ball bearing disintegrated. Never even stalled. And now. You—are—selling—me.*

Five days later, Roy and I made the official transaction at the new car dealership down the road from the used cars.

As I sat in my car for the last time, I created a scenario for this event. I imagined that my car never liked me in the first place, driving it a dull eighty miles a day between Ames and Des Moines. I imagined my car was confused, with most of its ample space always empty, its headlights politely viewing the interior of a garage, its truck frame never splattered with mud. Maybe my car tried to steal its keys and run away, get a canoe rack, and meet a more compatible driver.

It was ninety-three degrees outside, with humidity nearly as high. The new car lot had significantly more space than the wedge of the used car lot, as well as a glass-walled showroom. Not a single Iowan was interested in buying a new car on this stifling afternoon.

Roy, again in white slacks, but with a pink shirt, invited me into an office that wasn't his. Framed prints of prototype Hondas lined the wall. Near the door hung a magnetic board chronicling which salesmen sold which cars last month. Someone named Bill was in the number one slot, with fifteen gold Honda magnets.

While Roy completed paperwork, I observed four salesmen. They had nothing to do. Absolutely nothing. They all climbed into a minivan, one of two cars in the showroom. The other car was a 2001 Honda CRV, just like mine, but electric blue. There was a post-it note on the windshield that said, "sold." The salesmen in the minivan talked about their golf games and made jokes about who could or couldn't play eighteen holes in ninety-three degree weather. They looked comical, their identical slacked legs bent at sharp angles, their hips twisted so they could face each other. They engaged in an opinionated debate about whether or not kids should have to attend school in such hot weather. Although it was June, when most schools were done for the summer, Iowa's harsh winter meant extra days. One man claimed that kids couldn't learn if they had to fidget and sweat. Another asserted that he never got a day off due to the heat, and he turned out just fine. Another thought that most schools had air conditioning. Another said they didn't.

There were many forms to fill out, many places for my signature. Roy could have scripted the Constitution with his precise, smooth lines. My signature looked powerful. The slash of the "*J*," the fast slant and sweep of "*Hirt*," were drastically different than my father's heavy thick lines or my mother's careful cursive. I asked tentative questions, pretending that I knew what I was doing. But I didn't, so I shut up, signed there, dated there. I had no idea. No idea if the offer was fair, or the best, or if I would regret selling a car that, although it was expensive, was fairly useful. No idea how my parents would react.

I signed the final form. Roy took the keys. He cut me a check for four thousand dollars, the largest single amount of money I had ever received all at once. I placed the check and the paperwork into a blue folder which I slid into a faded denim backpack, the one I carried in high school, the one that was humming with good luck, keeping me together in this scary I-am-an-adult-I-can-sell-my-car-if-I-want-to moment.

"You want your license plates?" Roy stood up, was halfway out the door.

I was not expecting this question. I was suddenly coping with the fact that I hadn't planned a way back to my apartment, on the other side of town.

"You don't need them?"

"No. They're out-of-state."

He was right. They were Ohio plates. Three years in Iowa and I never bothered to switch.

I waited in the air-conditioned showroom and watched Roy remove the plates with a massive, blue, battery-powered screwdriver gun. I was trying to recall the summer bus schedule. My boyfriend was at work. He didn't even know I was here. Didn't really know I was selling my car today. I searched my pockets for quarters and dimes.

Roy handed me the plates. His face was wet. "Hot out there," he said.

"Sure is." I was aware that everything had halted. The salesmen in the minivan were silent, watching us. All the cars on the road paused at red lights. A phone rang softly in a back office, as if it knew no one would pick it up.

"You need a ride home?" Roy switched the screwdriver gun to his other hand. It was heavy. Then he held it with both hands, in front of his waist.

"What?"

"Home. I can give you a ride home." Roy's tone was polite but awkward, like he was trying to decide how to conclude our second date. I had the awful epiphany that he felt responsible for me.

"No thanks," I lied. "I've got some stuff to do on this side of town, then I'll catch the bus."

"Oh." Roy gave the slightest of nods, like a boy coming to terms with the girl who won't go out with him. He looked at the screwdriver gun.

Maynard Seeley, who introduced my grandparents to
each other, outside the greenhouses in June 1940

I felt horrible, instantly and completely. This was all a stupid mistake. All of it. These three years in Iowa, the car, my ethical aspirations not to depend on a car, my job and my quitting of the job, the fact that I'd told no one that I was selling my car, not my parents, not my boyfriend. Not even myself, in a way. Plus the fact that selling this car was an underhanded tactic to get back at my parents for divorcing. Now I had turned down Roy's nice offer for no reason other than my own bull-headed self-sufficiency. It was a million degrees outside; I was miles from my apartment. I had a four-thousand-dollar check but not three quarters for the bus. I had no clue what to do and I was concocting minor lies to cover for myself.

I was a bad liar. I felt like Roy didn't believe that I really wanted to wait for the bus. He might not have believed that I wanted to sell my car. For a moment, Roy's reaction merged with my image of my parents' disappointment. I was the angry daughter bullishly walking away with old license plates in a faded backpack, content to wait for the bus, determined to force my lie into truth, and I didn't need the help of a middle-aged salesman, and I didn't need my own car, and I was hurling my distrust at my broken parents, at money, at the whole world.

I considered shaking Roy's hand, invoking the classic symbol of a done deal, but he was holding the massive screwdriver. The way he held it, with both hands, suggested his life depended on not letting it go. He almost crouched against the wall, like I was scaring him. Maybe I was.

So I thanked Roy with a lie that was a smile, and walked out, into the searing high noon.

I hoped I would never see my car again, not in the used car lot with giant neon numbers taped to the window, not being driven across town by a stranger. I hoped I could forget it. I had yet to forget the Beretta. I hoped Roy could sell it quickly, so he wouldn't look at it day after day, wondering. I hoped I hadn't just made the mistake of a lifetime.

I glanced back once. I wanted to see what Roy was up to. He was leaning into the minivan, the one still filled with salesmen. One of them reached out, patting Roy on the shoulder. Perhaps it was Bill, Champion Salesman for May. Roy carefully set the screwdriver gun on the showroom floor. He stepped up into the minivan. His compatriots consoled him with promises of customers buying car after car in an endless, profitable stream. And maybe they teased him about all the women they had driven home, and maybe Roy blushed, but most likely he didn't. Then he probably drove my Honda up to the used car lot, handing it off to the mechanics who were wondering what to do with a used Volvo luggage rack.

I walked home.

A week later, a woman I had never met called me. She said her name was Maria. She explained she was considering buying my Honda. She was confused about why I had sold it, if it was in such good condition. Roy had given her my number.

"So there's nothing wrong with it?" she asked. From her tone I pegged her as mid-thirties, short brown hair, administrative assistant job, owned a cocker spaniel, liked diet colas.

"Nothing," I assured her, once, then twice. I gave her my going-to-school spiel. Then, before she could dig deeper, before I gave in to the temptation to recant and rant about *everything* that was *wrong*, I asked her why she was buying a used car.

A male voice answered. "My wife was in an accident last week. Totaled her CRV."

Apparently, Maria's husband had been listening. I thought it weird.

"Are you okay?" I asked. I pictured her brown hair hiding browner bruises. I wondered if she and the husband were in the same room, mouthing answers to each other.

"Banged up, nothing serious" she said. "I loved my CRV. I miss it. Yours is just like mine."

The husband concurred. He said he was surprised they'd found such a similar CRV.

"Oh." I paused. There were thousands of identical CRVs in the nation and I didn't fully understand what the husband was getting at. I waited. Something didn't feel right.

Maybe Roy was also listening, like this was some huge secret conference call meant to coerce a confession. Maybe everyone was listening— Roy, and Bill the Champion Salesman, and my parents, and the four salesman in the minivan, even the Volvo Man—waiting to hear how much money I'd scored, how much I was enjoying that four-thousand-dollar check, I, the spoiled, vindictive mastermind behind an elaborate scam.

"We're probably going to buy it," said the husband. "We just wanted to talk with the former owner. To make sure."

"Right," I said, "Makes sense." It didn't. It was a car, not a dog at the pound, not a child up for adoption. And they really had not asked me any worthwhile questions, and the husband had blown his cover by speaking, and it made no sense that there needed to be any level of covertness at all.

Then I said, "It's a great car. I would have kept it if I could have afforded it." I felt obligated to reassure these people.

Somehow, this was true enough for Maria and her husband. They could now fit me into the paradigm of their world, a world where anyone who could afford a car obviously owned one and loved it righteously, without reserve.

"That's a relief," said Maria.

"Yes," said the husband, "We were worried there was something, you know, really wrong with it."

I assumed they purchased it. I thought a lot about what I said to Maria. I would have kept the car if I could have afforded it. I think that was true enough for me, too. I sensed, for the first time, that *to afford* a car meant much more than being able to make the payments. There was something dangerous in keeping that car, something abstractly unaffordable, and it went beyond my mild activist intentions. The car had been from my parents. And now that they were splitting, I reverted to a deep anger, an anger that said *I will not take what you offer because you are ruining everything with this divorce.*

To say I could afford something also meant I had to consider the cost beyond the dollars. Months later, I attempted to chronicle the 47,000 miles, the approximately 783 hours I had driven in my Honda CRV. I could account for 31,650 miles, and my estimates were not exact but not conservative. I don't know what to conclude about this. I don't think I'm supposed to remember every mile, but it somehow seems a loss that those stretches of road, attached to so much time and money, attached to the expensive item my parents so wanted me to enjoy, are missing from my memory.

Ricinus Communis

I have a castor bean, mottled tan and brown, shiny like snakeskin, on my desk. The bean is a centimeter long and half a centimeter wide, with a coarse cap. The size (small) and beauty (unique) of the castor bean, Latin name *ricinus communis*, betray its contents. It is the source of the third most deadly toxin on the planet, a protein called ricin. Ranked with plutonium and botulism, a lethal dose of powdered ricin poisons irreversibly without a trace and marauds around the globe minus a vaccine. The danger is heightened by the ease of distilling ricin. All it takes is a packet of castor beans, acetone, lye, Epsom salts, a coffee grinder, and a strainer. Properly made and distributed, one gram of ricin can kill hundreds within twelve hours of exposure. Whenever I hear about ricin in the news, I'm amazed that the bean on my desk has the potential to be so sinister.

I'm astounded, too, by how the kin of my castor bean connect me to a duo of men: my father, who grew my bean and sold its relatives at the greenhouse; and Ken Olsen, the third person in the history of the nation brought to trial for possession of ricin. He made the ricin from castor beans he bought from my father, and he may have been plotting to kill his wife.

Where does this odd tale begin? Does its heart beat with the bean or in the disgruntled motivations of Ken Olsen? Do I start with Olsen's trial and my handwritten notebook about the tactics of post-9/11 federal prosecutors juxtaposed with the baffling inadequacy of Olsen's defense? Or do I start with the sketchy political motivations attributed to my father, and how the FBI came calling under the auspices of the Patriot Act, investigating the connection between a small-time greenhouse owner and a would-be poisoner?

It is perhaps best to start by explaining how events led Ken Olsen to be the fourth corner in the square of me, my dad, and castor beans.

Ken Olsen lived in Spokane, Washington, married since 1975, three kids, and twenty-five years as a software designer at Agilent Technologies. In 1999, Olsen had an affair with his massage therapist. To cover up, Olsen pursued massage therapy as a second job. He kept up the affair for a year. In 2000, the other woman left him because Olsen wouldn't leave his wife.

My father's cameo begins here. As he remembers Valentine's Day of 2000, Hirt's Greenhouse was enjoying its usual run of rose-red profit. An online order for a couple packets of castor beans, placed at midnight, drew little attention. The next morning, he mailed the beans to a post office box in Spokane. In March, my father filled a second order for the same customer. Two years later he'd have to explain the orders to the FBI, a future predicament quite unprecedented for a third-generation greenhouse manager expecting inquiries about houseplants, not inquiries about ingredients for biological weapons.

Olsen was buying more than castor beans online; he also purchased the military's patented recipe for ricin, which he bought on a CD-ROM from Kurt Saxon, an Arkansas author of separatist writings. The CD-ROM was titled *The Poor Man's James Bond*, one of Saxon's bestsellers

Dad outside his parents' backyard greenhouse, circa 1983

on how to subvert the system on pennies a day or how to build the gadgets of the secret and the wealthy in your basement. It's easy to look at Olsen's online purchases in 2000 and assume that he was planning to kill his wife so he could be with his mistress.

But then, in late 2000, the massage therapist rekindled her affair with Olsen, even though he hadn't fulfilled her ultimatum to leave his wife for good. Whatever he had been planning would wait.

All was quiet until July of 2001, a long-ago summer suitably labeled *before*. The affair had reached a critical point, again, and again, Olsen would not leave his wife. The massage therapist bailed, again.

One day at work, shortly after the break-up, Olsen downloaded and printed a 150-page document about explosives. A manager noticed it and called the police. Olsen claimed it was research for his son's Boy Scout project. Agilent Technologies fired him almost immediately and had guards escort him from the building. They did not let him clean out his cubicle.

When a supervisor boxed Olsen's personal belongings, the contents of a locked drawer proved even more alarming: books with incriminating titles, *How to Kill* and *Getting Even,* volumes 1 and 2; a turkey baster and measuring cups; test tubes; acetone and Epsom salts; a baggie of castor beans; and a waxy white powder in a Tropicana juice bottle stoppered with a wad of paper towel. The police confiscated the items. No one knew what the white powder could be; they just knew it had nothing to do with software.

On September 6, 2001, after the Washington State Crime Lab concluded they had no way to confirm what the substance was, the police passed the items to FBI Agent Joseph Cleary of the Joint Terrorism Task Force. Cleary had been on the force for a mere twenty-four hours. He had no idea what he was about to face.

There is coincidence of the highest kind here. My dad, involved in his own affair with no easy way out, sells castor beans to a guy who thinks there's no easy way out of his affair. The first transaction, Valentine's Day 2000, happens the week my mom discovers my dad's affair; the second transaction happens the week my mom calls to tell me about the affair. Can I admit that it's a dark parallel?

Another fearful symmetry: Olsen's mysterious white powder in a juice bottle finds its way to national crime labs five days before September 11. It means that no one at the United States Army Medical Research Institute of Infectious Diseases (USAMRIID) gets around to analyzing the powder until November 2001, because they are busy with a mess of things, including another white powder, the anthrax sent to Senator Tom Daschle, a Florida tabloid, and NBC studios.

Olsen's white powder turns out to be 19 percent ricin, a crude mixture but only possible with the aid of intentional distillation. The Feds prepare charges, but again, post-9/11, things are different. Before, the Feds would have had to prove that Olsen not only made the ricin, but that he had a clear, direct target. After 9/11, Patriot Act in hand, prosecutors only had to prove that he had ricin. Whether he had specific plans to use it became, oddly, irrelevant. What could have been a low-profile case of poor judgment became a high-profile federal case, a bioweapons trial, with a handful of castor beans from Hirt's Greenhouse at the core.

And a final irony: The terrorist attacks would spawn the legislation that would help to incriminate Olsen, but those same attacks created an unprecedented delay in the forthcoming charges against Olsen. While the FBI juggled national security and orange alerts, Olsen lived at home with his wife, the wife that lawyers would later argue he wanted to kill. He was arrested on June 18, 2002, and charged with possession of a biological weapon with intent to harm—almost a year after the discovery of his ricin.

The FBI called my dad in August, 2002, and asked him to confirm some transaction records. "The castor beans are big sellers," he told FBI agent Leland McEuen, and when he repeated the conversation to me, I heard nothing but pride in his voice. "The FBI was very nice," he said, knowing full well he had the legal right to sell castor beans. My dad spoke with that haughty confidence suggesting he was pleased to thwart "the Man" via his routine sales of a potentially harmful toxin.

In January 2003, the prosecutors subpoenaed him to testify in the forthcoming trial. The news of his subpoena was the first I'd heard about the incident. The final chance piece of the irony puzzle fell into place. At the time, I lived in Moscow, Idaho, just eighty miles south of Spokane, where the trial would be held. I could attend. I cleared my schedule.

My dad's reaction to the subpoena was mixed. He resented the FBI's snooping (blaming all of 9/11 on their ineptitude, calling me frequently with excoriating rants against all involved), but he worried that the case would bode badly for innocent horticulturists who appreciated castor beans. Dad was excited to have an all-expense paid trip west, and he was raving about the unusual aspects of Ken Olsen's dark life, gleaned through Google searches. My dad always wanted to be a lawyer, and with his own ongoing divorce, after-hours litigation had almost become a hobby. He had an affinity with the troublemakers. He had his suspicions.

Back in Spokane, Olsen's wife, Carol, took an odd step. She acknowledged the affair and then defended her husband's actions, claiming he was making castor oil for his massage practice and that the FBI was on an out-of-control, post-attack witch hunt. Perhaps in response, to make it clear that this was no smalltime game, the prosecutors leveled a second charge, possession of a chemical weapon with intent to harm.

Unfortunately, my dad's planned testimony got nixed just a few weeks after the subpoena. He was distraught and worked up, edgy over the fact that his name and Hirt's Greenhouse were now in an FBI file, but he wouldn't get to testify to correct any misinterpretations about his peripheral involvement. I realized that was the reason why they probably cut his appearance; any FBI agent half worth his psychological-profiling training would easily see that my dad could be a difficult witness, especially when forced to testify for people he saw as the bad guys.

I promised him I'd attend anyway, not only to see how the Hirt's Greenhouse connection would surface, but to lay eyes on a man who made ricin, another man caught having an affair like my father, yet on a path so much more malevolent. Olsen's perplexing narrative intrigued me. Why would the typical American suburban man decide to make ricin, a toxin so powerful not even military labs knew how to deal with it? What could have been so awful about his home life, so tempting about the other woman, the affair, the deception?

Such a little thing, the castor bean. Such chaos beneath its smooth shell, where the white pulp naturally contains miniscule protein chains that, when distilled and ingested, can dissolve a circulatory system in twelve hours. Its existence, like Pandora's Box costumed as Pandora's Bean, reminds me how close chaos reigns. How odd that Kenneth Olsen stepped beyond the idea of ricin into the realm of possession and intent. How intriguing that under the shelter of a Midwest greenhouse, my father sells castor beans to anyone, anywhere, as long as the blinking speed of credit approval seals the transaction.

The plants and seeds are botanically interesting and perfectly legal. Lots of people grow them. Picture one castor bean plant, stunning doublestar leaves and arching stems, some as tall as twelve feet, and the tantalizing clusters of shiny seeds, a presence like a dragon lording over the land of botany. They grow wild in warmer regions, and expansive fields shimmer in the California sun. When harvested, their oil ends up in the infamous laxative, and also as a cheap lubricant for machinery. The husks and leaves and stems, purged of their valuable oil but not their troublesome toxin, can be detoxified with a heat treatment and then trucked to livestock yards for hungry cattle. Castor bean plants are an excellent crop for an industrialized society that runs on meat and machines. They'd be perfect, were it not for the one lectin protein, the ricin, that makes them indisputably deadly.

My father started growing castor beans with a mix of curiosity and controversy. He knew the mature plants were bizarrely beautiful, he knew the seeds held concentrated loads of ricin, he knew customers would want the plants for either reason, and he knew he was only obligated to sell, not to ask questions. Savvy and more than willing to sell strange stuff, he offered the plants and seeds at the greenhouse and online through the website and Ebay auctions, never imagining that one morning the FBI would question him about one customer, one purchase, one transaction, that led to three grams of ricin in one cubicle, far away. And even if the thought had crossed his mind, my dad is the type of transgressor who would go ahead and sell castor beans anyway, almost as a challenge. They've always been a favorite of the fringe, symbols on the estates of the disgruntled.

The case of the *United States of America v. Olsen* opened July 1, 2003, earning blurbs on the national morning news shows and the AP wire. I saw it on the CNN ticker as I ate my breakfast at 5:30 AM, before making the eighty-three-mile commute on a two-lane road through the burnished wheat fields of eastern Washington, tracking the Idaho border, emerging from the high plains to twist through pine forests into the city of Spokane. I clutched a new blank notebook and walked like a nervous fool to the steps of the courthouse.

I had worked as a journalist previously, so I had an idea of how to document this event. Mostly, though, I was a creative writer, fairly intent on subverting "facts" rather than reporting them, addicted to narrative and anti-narratives, two-thirds of the way through my MFA. I didn't know what to expect from the federal trial, or even from myself. Would I have to explain why I was there? Would the testimony be hard to follow?

Would this trial last for months and months? How rusty were my journalism skills? What was I going to do with this bizarre narrative thrust into my path?

Of all the unknowns I tried to anticipate on my drive up to Spokane, I hadn't anticipated the perpetual yellow alert status of the security guards at the courthouse, four at the main entrance and two more in the hall outside the courtroom. One step through the metal detector and an old guard pulled me aside, wondering what I was doing with a Gameboy and cell phone in my bag. Didn't I know about the ban on electronics? Hadn't I watched the news recently? He nodded toward a placard on an easel. Trimmed in stoplight yellow, it listed the specifics of a nation on alert. There was a bullet point about being vigilant for electronics doubling as detonators. He wrote my name on appropriately yellow sticky notes, thumbing them onto my electronics. He bundled the phone and the Gameboy with a rubber band and set them in a drawer crammed with other gadgets.

Another guard requested my driver's license, tilting it for hints of fraud. He quizzed me about where I was headed in the nine-story building, then pointed me to the elevators. At the ninth floor, the next duo of guards confiscated my water bottle and my newspaper. No liquids. No reading material. I relinquished, held my breath, and they nodded me through one more metal detector. Cleared. I entered the courtroom, the sanctum, windowless with high ceilings, not huge but not tiny, seats like pews in a church of judgment. I spotted Olsen's wife, Carol, in the front row. I sat in the back row.

Ken Olsen arrived with his handlers, two federal marshals. They escorted him to his seat between his public defenders, gray-haired John Clark, frumpy in a two-toned suit, and Tina Hunt, her shoulders broad as a batter's, conspicuous under her black dress which had a wispy white scarf sewn into place. Olsen's navy suit and tie suggested ease and confidence, but his face, pale and tight over a clenched jaw, was a portrait of anxiety. He flipped papers and bent his ear to whispers from his lawyers.

He smiled fleetingly at Carol. Yesterday, at a press conference, she had announced that she would not take the stand in her husband's defense, yet she was standing by him without reservation. Reacting to the press conference stunt, Judge Neilsen had requested she not talk to reporters during the trial, since she was refusing to testify. So the front row was where I'd see her for the next three weeks, sometimes with her four children, all in their teens and twenties and good-looking as movie stars; sometimes with her father, a retired military man who took notes; and sometimes by herself.

I was relieved that she was not allowed to talk to me. I was worried she would want to know who I was and why I was perched at the back, taking tons more notes than the reporters. I didn't know how to begin to explain. Was I here out of fascination? How morbid. How inappropriate. Was it obligation? But to what. My last name? Was I here to glean more fodder for distrusting the government?

Opening arguments began with United States Assistant Attorney Stephanie Whitaker, petite, blonde, professional-chic in high heels. Her voice was hushed and trained. Even the surveillance cameras paused to hear the nuances.

"This man appears normal," she said, enunciating each syllable with the skill of a performer. Olsen was behind her so she turned to face him, saw that he was not watching her, then tilted her face back to the microphone. "But there's a side no one knows." The jurors cautiously opened their notebooks, pens poised. Like a narrator for a true-crime primetime news magazine show, she listed the Internet search strings the FBI uncovered on Olsen's computer. *Poison. Ricin. Undetectable. How to kill. Killing without a trace.* Incrimination lingered in the calculated pauses. She might as well have been whispering *"guilty."*

When defense attorney John Clark took the podium, he played the 9/11 card as if he held nothing but aces. "We were different then," he said, meaning *then* as August 2001, the month of the ricin discovery, as compared to *now*, the summer of 2003. He was asking the jurors for what may have been impossible, to see the evidence through a pre-terror attack lens. Clark continued with the rationale for an acquittal. Olsen was just trying to make castor oil to fulfill his "irresponsible sense of curiosity," a curiosity fueled by Boy Scout merit badges and massage techniques. When the oil dried, the residue contained crude ricin, and

Olsen meant to throw it away but he forgot. So what the government called a biological weapon the defense called a byproduct. The timing of the affair was coincidental, what Clark called "a very human mistake."

And then, Clark took sideways aim at the Patriot Act with its new interpretation about possession and intent. He reminded the courtroom that possessing ricin was, technically, not illegal, only possessing it with *intent to harm* was illegal. And Olsen, Clark pointed out, had not harmed anyone, nor was there solid evidence of intent. If the word *guilty* traipsed in the pauses of the prosecution's opening argument, the word *circumstantial* flashed during the defense's opening arguments. Evidence culled from the chaos of Google searches? A nation in fear of white powders? Enemies of the state, from Spokane to Afghanistan? Clark jabbed at the government's mentality. "To those who only have a hammer, everything begins to look like a nail."

"We all have things in our homes that could be used as weapons," he said, pausing for effect, but the effect was lost as he fumbled in his pocket and lost his place on his yellow legal pad, flipping pages and admitting he was mixed up. "But that doesn't mean we will use them," he concluded, allowing a measured glance to the trio that made up the prosecution: Whitaker, her co-attorney Earl Hicks, whose very presence spoke of long hours hashing out the intricacies of incriminating wrong-doers, and young FBI Agent Joseph Cleary, clean-cut and sitting patriot-straight, assisting in his first bioweapons case.

With opening arguments finished, the first of forty-four witnesses—none of which would be Olsen or his wife—took the stand.

The castor bean is a *seed* misnamed *bean* for its oval shape. The first half of its name, *castor*, adds to the confusion. Amateur gardeners might assume since so many plant names connect to the daytime celebrities of Greek mythology that the castor bean takes its name from Castor, one of Leda's twin sons possibly born from the rape perpetrated by Zeus in swan form. The metaphorical possibilities are perfect. Castor and his twin Pollux were cast into the midnight as the constellation Gemini, the twins of light and dark, of lust and violence, namesaked in a gorgeous plant whose seeds can be both cathartic and harmful. Too bad that's not the case. Instead, Mary Durant points out in her book *Who Named the Daisy? Who Named the Rose?* that the plant takes its name from the Greek word for *beaver*. The soggy genius of dams and log piles was known to the Greeks as *kastor*, from the Sanskrit *kasturi* for musk. Beaver musk was cathartic. So was the oil from the strange new seed.

The etymology of *ricin* is even less interesting. It is merely a shortening of the plant's Latin moniker, *ricinus communis*. It debuted in medical dictionaries at the end of the nineteenth century, when scientists identified the lectin protein, the poisonous one, and had to name it. The pronunciation of *ricin* is notable—the first syllable rhyming with *cry*; the second a homophone of *sin*. Say it softly. Louder. It defies enunciation. It is the sound of jilted love. It is the sound of blood making its last pulsing rush.

How did anyone look at the seed and end up with such a powerful biotoxin? It's tough to say for sure. Documents on the true origins of state-sponsored biological warfare are shredded or seriously confidential or complete lies or not available to graduate students in Idaho. One heady source is the book *Castor*, an English translation of the USSR's agricultural exploits in the early years of the twentieth century. For three hundred mind-numbing pages, V. A. Moshkin and a few of his peers report the minutest details of castor cultivation. *Flowering of. Pollination of. Seed Ripening of. Soil Preparation for. Cytology and Genetics of.* Page after musty page of tiny charts and tables with numbers stretching behind decimal points. Hurrah, hurrah for the Soviets, whose astute farming would provide the world with an abundance of castor oil.

And then, seven pages—two percent of the book—about ricin, wherein Moshkin notes that the toxicity of the ricin protein is reduced when the plant grows in very hot climates. A cooler, controlled climate, with plenty of water, allows the seed to become highly toxic. His awareness of the horrific symptoms of ricin poisoning is appropriately obtuse. "The toxin is a protein of the globular type. It is capable of causing agglutination of suspension of erythrocytes." Translation: It dissolves circulatory systems.

So, if Olsen were planning to poison his wife, and if he did it by somehow getting her to inhale and ingest the ricin, within twelve hours his wife's retinas would hemorrhage. Her throat would burn. Her stomach would churn and expel whatever she'd eaten, and her colon would convulse continuously. She would see blood and mucus in her diarrhea because the ricin would be shutting down her intestinal walls while also exploding her red blood cells. By day two, she'd be in shock due to dehydration. Her vision would blur, her heart would jitter as if the chambers were trying to separate. By day three, the ricin would ransack all her organs and she'd die. An autopsy would reveal massive circulatory failure, the cause undetectable.

Moshkin's numbers in the tables about the toxicity of ricin do their job of masking. It is impossible to glean any details about the experiments the Soviets must have conducted. On what, on whom? Where? *What did the Soviets know?*

Enter the United States and World War II. 1944. At President Roosevelt's request, the newly formed Biological Warfare Committee received $250,000. With the money, the military built research centers at Fort Detrick, Maryland; Horn Island, Mississippi; and Granite Peak, Utah. The research centers focused on chemical agents, infectious agents, and ricin's trippy 'hood, the toxins.

Fort Detrick got the go-ahead for decoding ricin. The military had heard of it, but beyond a name and its deadly potential, they knew nothing. *The United States and Biological Warfare* reports that Proctor and Gamble got involved, concluding that not only was ricin as powerful as botulism, but, as an economic bonus in trying times, it would be cheap to produce. The boys at P&G really wanted the government to award them the ricin contract. However, the military had already gone ahead with a few random ricin experiments at Mississippi's Horn Island, a 4,154 acre landscape of sand dunes. When they realized that ricin could be carried ashore via coastal winds to Biloxi, they halted plans for mass production and testing. The big obstacle was the fact that ricin poisoning had no vaccine and no cure. Someone must have had a glimmer of foresight when considering that any mishap would make Fort Detrick appear catastrophically inept. Scared of their own potential for devastation, the researchers quietly pushed ricin aside and turned their attentions to anthrax.

By the seventh witness on the second day, I felt like an expert in corporate security strategies, because the prosecution was using reams of workday data to try to prove Olsen's intentions. Agilent Technologies imposed rigorous control over its employees and stored their online activities in what amounted to an electronic gate guarded by St. Peter. This proved handy for the prosecution. Microchip ID cards tracked arrivals and exits. Internet proxy logs stored every website visited, every pop-up ad encountered, every print job and email and search string. The proxy logs so excited Stephanie Whitaker that she claimed, "we have captured a thought process. We have his pattern, his progression. This is as close as we can get to getting into someone's mind."

If anyone else in the courtroom was as unnerved by this presumption as I was, I couldn't tell, which worried me. If computers represented thought processes, we were all guilty of something. How many Internet searches had I conducted, that, if I did something questionable in the future, could be used against me? Enough. *To those who have a hammer, everything begins to look like a nail.*

The implications worried me. But then came Witness Number 14, Kurt Saxon, via a video recorded in March, before the trial encountered delays, and a vast new set of concerns besieged me.

White-haired Saxon, seventy-one, had been allowed to testify by video due to poor health. He owned Atlan Formularies in Alpena, Arkansas, a "company" that sold "information" on "how to do everything your grandparents did around the house." He, like my father, had sold Olsen one thing he needed for ricin—the government's recipe, concocted back in the nineteen-forties at Fort Detrick.

In the pre-recorded video testimony, the camera was unmoving; the lighting, jaundiced. The lawyers questioned from somewhere off screen, and Judge Neilsen conducted the proceedings via a teleconferencing hook-up which someone else was videotaping in Spokane. The splices and edits were amateur. Not nearly as exciting as live courtroom action.

Saxon leaned back in his chair as he testified about one of his best sellers, *Granddad's Wonderful Book of Electricity*, and the ever-popular *Poor Man's James Bond* (PMJB) CD-ROM series. The PMJB, which Saxon confirmed that Olsen purchased from him, taught "improvised weaponry." Saxon wrote all the material himself, and was pleased to announce that the four-volume PMJB had recently expanded to a fifth volume.

"Volume three is very specific about making ricin," he affirmed, flashing back into a story about how he simply asked the military for their ricin recipe, claimed that he received it without hassle, and had been filling the orders of the disenfranchised ever since. Without hesitation he explained the function of the acetone (removes the castor oil) and the Epsom salts (forces the ricin to the bottom of a mixture, so the nontoxic liquid can be easily discarded). But he felt that only trained chemists could make true weapons-grade ricin.

Yet Saxon, eager to test the military's recipe, had actually made ricin, and he talked about it under oath, either oblivious to or dismissive of the Patriot Act. A prosecutor asked him why he had made ricin. "Because it's interesting," he answered. He asserted that he would never actually use it, not even on a cat, not even in conjunction with his strong dislike of the CIA. The jurors chuckled.

He added that he'd gotten a call from an unsatisfied customer. The ricin apparently "just made the victim throw up." Saxon's back-up advice? "Hit them with a brick." *Ricin failing you? Hit them with a brick!* It became a phrase I bandied about all week.

Creepy though he was, I rather liked Saxon. I think the jurors did, too. They grinned at each other, grins that said, *Well now, here's a character! Can you believe this guy?* Their laughter startled me. If Saxon had testified in person, I bet only raised eyebrows would have played on the jurors' faces. Video testimony radically altered the dynamics of the courtroom. It's easy to laugh at someone who won't ever know you laughed at him. While the jurors laughed, the lawyers weren't even paying attention. They'd seen the video plenty of times, and there was no need to take careful notes or plan a cross or recross of new questions.

In the back row, which I was coming to think of as *my back row,* I filled my ninth page of handwritten notes. I realized I was enamored with the situation because Saxon was claiming precisely what Olsen was claiming. Both admitted to making ricin. Both asserted they never intended to use it on anyone. Olsen's lawyers defended him with the notion of irresponsible curiosity. Saxon thought "interesting" was reason enough. Olsen was on trial; Saxon, after his testimony, got to refill his coffee and head home to his next set of fifty-dollar orders for the PMJB series. The disparity added another twist to my insides. Why was the government so keen on prosecuting Ken Olsen, but not Kurt Saxon? And why did Saxon's brazen bravado seem so much more appealing than Olsen's agreement not to testify on his own behalf?

Listening to Saxon got me thinking about perspective. Put Olsen's case in perspective, and it's not much. His case toddles next to the giants of ricin legend.

In two infamous and dramatic cases often reported in biological weapon literature, the dissident Bulgarian writer Vladimir Kostov, in exile in London, was sickened, but not killed, by a ricin attack in 1978. Ten days later, Kostov's fellow radical writer, Georgi Markov, also exiled to London, was killed with ricin. An assassin jabbed Markov with an umbrella tip doubling as a pellet gun. The assassin had injected Markov with a lethal dose of ricin. Meanwhile, Kostov heard about Markov's strange demise and recalled receiving a similar mysterious jab, followed by an inexplicable fever. An autopsy of Markov and an examination of Kostov revealed that each writer had a tiny pellet lodged beneath the jab wound. But Kostov's pellet had lodged in fat, and therefore the ricin hadn't been fully released. For 1978, the pellets were notably advanced and devilishly clever. The attempts, perpetrated in London, left Scotland Yard flummoxed about how to proceed.

The CIA was shrugging as well. In 1980, Boris Korczak, a CIA double agent, died the same way, via ricin pellet assassination, in Tysons Corners, Virginia. A colossal argument rose between the Soviets and the CIA over the circumstances of Korczak's posthumous future. In the end, a compromise was reached. The CIA kept the ricin pellet, and the Soviets ferried Korczak's body back to the homeland. Various sources report "other assassinations" involving ricin in the states, but the details never emerge from between the lines. No names, no dates, no suggestions.

I think that the government went after Olsen because they could, because the irony of Olsen's situation is that in an attempt to distill an undetectable poison, he left a very detectable online paper trail.

When FBI Agents Cleary and McEuen took the stand, they did so with laptops and binders marking a sometimes minute-by-minute progression of what they called Olsen's online activity, synonymous with *thought process*, if you asked the prosecutors. As the first week of testimony recessed for the holiday break, I realized that Olsen's decision not to testify was a colossal mistake. By not speaking, he was letting the Internet speak for him. He was letting the prosecution get away with saying that his Google searches were "in his own words," and that they were also his *only words*. How much easier to prosecute the silent, I realized.

Agent Joseph Cleary's four hours of Monday-morning testimony revealed the thudding dullness of day-to-day FBI work. No Agent Mulder and *X-Files*, no witty *Law and Order* investigators. Stephanie Whitaker walked him through every minute facet of his involvement in the case. *What were the items found in Olsen's cubicle? How many items were there? Did you put them in separate containers? When did you send them to USAMRIID? When did USAMRIID respond? How did they respond? Is this a photograph of the items you sent to USAMRIID?*

Because he was the FBI, he was allowed to have his laptop on the stand, to doublecheck his facts. *No wonder Olsen was reluctant to testify*, I thought to myself. His day on the stand would have pitted his word against the credentials and hard drive of the FBI. It would have been his (probably) soft and "aw-shucks" voice against the trained-dog authority of Agent Cleary. It would have been the inexplicable narrative of Ken Olsen juxtaposed against the cast-in-stone criminal narrative used by the prosecution. Chaos versus an established pattern. That verdict has been in for a long time.

When would my father have testified? Maybe on the day Saxon testified, since it was the CD-ROM from Saxon and the castor beans from my father that gave Olsen the two starting points. Or maybe he would have testified in the midst of FBI agent testimony. I decided to subpoena him for my own tangential questioning.

I asked him for his honest appraisal of the fact that he had sold, was selling, and would continue to sell a product that, in the wrong hands, was so uniquely poisonous. He hardly paused before responding, "Drug stores sell Drano, and you can kill people with that."

It was the type of response I should have expected. One that absolved blame, and that displaced blame, one rife with some sort of fallacy of association. The usual. True, Drano could kill. However, Drano had a practical purpose, whereas ricin, in the context of Ken Olsen, did not appear to have a practical purpose. Furthermore, Drano poisoning could be halted and averted, not pleasantly, but ricin poisoning was guaranteed to dissolve blood cells in a matter of hours and lead to a sure death. Drano is detectable. Ricin is not.

I wondered about my dad's moral leanings in relation to the tendencies of someone like Kenneth Olsen. My father was hardly an extremist. He wasn't a member of a militia or a lone wolf. Neither was Olsen. But my dad was certainly on some sort of fringe, and his fringe seemed to be landscaped with castor bean plants, which he had planted in the front yard of his pricey house in the dignified Ledgewood community of Strongsville.

Years ago, he had claimed that the government was behind the Oklahoma City bombing, that McVeigh was the fall guy for a major conspiracy. In fact, shortly after the bombing, my father pointed to a towering stack of bagged lawn fertilizer, a mixture of potassium, nitrogen, and phosphorous, and told me the same stuff was in the rental truck that drove the bomb to the doorstep of the federal building. He was furious after 9/11, claiming that President Bush knew exactly what was planned, that the government did not immediately ground all air traffic because they wanted to see what else would happen. Was it, I wondered, the beginnings of paranoia? His fear for thinking this stuff, or mine for conflating his baseless opinions into something more.

But his was also the type of response that denied a moral distinction between weapons, a feeling that lingered with me long after our conversation. By comparing ricin to Drano, my dad was trying to tell me the weapon didn't matter. What mattered was the intent to kill. But again, my dad was deflecting responsibility. He was essentially saying, *I don't matter in this drama. I just sold him the castor beans. He would have found some other way to accomplish his goal.* True, to a point. I recalled Kurt Saxon and his earlier advice for best-laid plans gone wrong. The brick if not the ricin, right?

Perhaps what I was after with my father was some admission of long-term consequences, some awareness that he thought beyond greenhouse profit and the titillating idea of poison. Or just some hint he was not planning on stocking the *Poor Man's James Bond* a shelf above *The Backyard Rose Garden*, just for kicks. And I knew I was anxious over what the FBI might conclude about my father, because I saw how adept they were at crushing Olsen. What they had was more than a hammer, more than a brick.

Who reads stuff like the *Poor Man's James Bond?* People who are bored, people who are disillusioned with the steady routine of the average American life. And, of course, people who are poor or middle class, yet aspire to the tricks and gadgets of the wealthy. Batman and his butler, Alfred, and Bond and Q, for example.

When Olsen's girlfriend testified, she succinctly placed Ken Olsen in the readership of the *PMJB*. She testified that even after Ken agreed to marriage counseling to calm Carol, he wrote covert messages requesting they "find a way to communicate that will not be easy to track without anyone's knowledge." He wanted anonymity, or at least an alter-ego. The girlfriend said that he often signed his letters YPFF, code for *your punctilious forever friend*. "Precise in behavior" is the definition I bet he intended for *punctilious*. Amusingly, she claimed she never knew what the word meant. Precise behavior indeed, but to what end, when the object of affection doesn't get it?

By the middle of the second week, the pace of the trial stalled as the prosecution went forth with nine USAMRIID witnesses in video testimony format, on video not because of illness, as was Saxon's case, but because matters of national security prevented them from leaving Fort Detrick. So, again, the motionless camera focused, the weak lighting appeared yellow, and disembodied voices asked the most mundane questions ever, and everyone in the courtroom stared at monitors. This witness received the packages each day. This witness logged the packages.

This witness decided what level of biohazard safety to employ. This witness scraped powder. This witness was an idiot and mixed up the identification numbers on some of the baggies. This witness caught the mistake. As the tape rolled, all the lawyers appeared deeply engaged in other things. For them, the testimony was the equivalent of summer reruns.

Throughout all this numbingly lethargic testimony, an older man in gray slacks and a trim black windbreaker slept in front of me, in the second row. He wore glasses. His black and white hair was cropped. Each day, he paid attention for an hour or so, then folded his arms, slouched just enough to support his head, and napped. He did not snore, drool, or nod into moments of deeper sleep. His eyes were barely closed. Bored with the video, I watched the long rise and fall of his chest, contemplating how screwy it was to be here at this moment.

Meanwhile, aware that no one was really paying attention to anything, Ken Olsen, at one moment, mouthed something to Carol. They were not allowed to talk, really, but this one communication slipped past the jar-headed federal marshals. Later, during a break, I heard Carol tell a friend who had just arrived that "Ken is wearing his Goofy socks today. For good luck. They are the ones I sent him in jail." Goofy socks? Did I hear her right? I was petrified to ask. The prosecution had bioweapons experts on the docket; the defense had Goofy socks.

Eventually, we came to the agent who called Hirt's Greenhouse, Leland McEuen. He had an oversized binder that held Olsen's entire Internet proxy log. Somewhere in there was a visit to www.hirts.com, one midnight on a distant Valentine's Day.

The mention of Hirt's Greenhouse, when it came, was brief, exciting, and earned the marginalia of stars and three exclamation points in my notes. Agent McEuen confirmed that "yes" Olsen had most likely purchased castor beans from *www.hirts.com*. That's all there really was to say about it. Yet my heart thumped. What was so exciting was that no one knew a Hirt was sitting in the courtroom. I felt like a spy. It was a great day and that evening I called my father to tell him Hirt's Greenhouse had ten seconds of mention in the nation's third-ever ricin trial, and I'd been there to hear it.

I replayed the moment for him, and he listened intently. He wanted to know when Olsen would testify. When I told him Olsen wasn't on the witness list, hadn't even spoken a public word since his arrest, my father was dumbfounded.

The trial wound down with a whimper once the prosecution rested their case. The defense needed just two days for their witnesses. My high hopes for a stellar defense, one that would shut down the federal steamroller, drooped when the star witness for the defense, Vanderbilt chemistry professor Thomas Harris, couldn't do much better than point out the "one in a thousand" chance of USAMRIID's weight measurements all ending in zero, which they apparently did.

The defense tried to use Harris to cast doubt on the reliability of USAMRIID's testing, a peculiar decision since Harris had unsuccessfully testified for the defense in 2001 at the nation's second-ever ricin trial, where Dr. Ray Mettetal, a Vanderbilt colleague of Harris', was initially found guilty of possessing ricin with intent to harm. In reality, the defense didn't have a large selection of expert pro-ricin witnesses. The government, after all, was on a winning streak.

Family friends testified that Ken Olsen was a peaceful man, loved his family, worked hard. But on cross-examination, the friends admitted they knew nothing of his ricin research, and were surprised at his arrest. *Get him on the stand*, I imagined myself telling Tina Hunt, should she care to seek my counsel. *Make him explain himself. Require him to defend his actions against this juggernaut of government.* I couldn't begin to imagine how Olsen was just able to sit there with his hands under the table and his Goofy socks pulled up snugly.

I saved my hope for the moment Olsen's private investigator, Tom Krzyzank, took the stand as a last-chance witness to go head to head with the slew of formal experts. Tina Hunt presented an actual bottle of castor oil. Kyzyzank said he'd purchased a bottle like that at a grocery store and another at a nutrition store. He mentioned the price and gave the cost difference between buying castor oil and making castor oil. It wasn't significant. Hunt squared her shoulders and said that was all she had for the witness. The strategy confounded me. I could not decipher

her intent. Why such a weak defense? Why was Ken Olsen even in the courtroom? I felt like I was suddenly watching a Pinter play, assailed with non sequitors.

The final witness in *USA v. Olsen* was Rex Walker, a family friend and gentle-giant guy who said *"oh lord"* and *"darndest."* "Oh Lord, I'm doing my darndest to understand what's happened to my very good friend." On cross-examination, he maintained that none of this changed his opinion about Ken Olsen. Not a bit of it.

He was trying very hard not to cry. His brief testimony made me realize that the testimony of the defense witnesses felt so futile because it was, well, absolutely futile. The prosecution could summon science to prove the purity and the weight of the ricin; they were allowed to have binders upon binders of Internet proxy logs; the FBI agents were allowed to consult documents on their notebook computers as they testified. The defense, left to defend whatever Ken Olsen was up to, was left with the losing ticket, a defense of the decidedly unscientific chaos, amplified by the silence of the accused.

In the closing arguments, Tina Hunt used a prop to try to show why the ricin Olsen made was not potent enough to kill, referencing a claim by Dr. Harris. The prop was a large gold chain with a dog-toy ball at one end and an inflated blue rubber glove at the other. Hunt disconnected a chain link in the middle to illustrate that the chains of protein could break, and therefore be less potent. I had no idea what the ball and glove symbolized, and she didn't explain them. The prosecution, meanwhile, had prepared a PowerPoint presentation, but the clerk could not get Whitaker's computer to transmit it to the juror's monitors. So she just revisited her opening argument drama. She added this kicker, however: "Either USAMRIID is wrong, or the defendant purified [his ricin]. Which one makes more sense?" The question lingered in the air, twisting itself into permutations that made me angry because I resented Whitaker's assumption that she got to impose a definition on *sense*. I didn't wait around for the verdict.

My father still sells castor beans at the greenhouse. Ken Olsen, however, won't be grinding poison anytime soon. On July 17, 2003,

the jury took just four hours to find him guilty for possession of a biological weapon with intent to harm and possession of a chemical weapon
with intent to harm. He faced life sentences for both charges, but ended
up with thirteen years and nine months. He'll be free just in time for
his sixties, in 2017. His lawyers are appealing. His wife and children
have dried their eyes and ducked from the media spotlight. I've shelved
my notebook from those three weeks in the world of law, and I toy with
the idea of contacting Olsen in prison.

I would tell him what I think his defense failed to argue thoroughly: Just because pieces fit into a pattern does not make the pattern
accurate. Patterns are an attempt to compensate for chaos, to catch what
might spill from Pandora's box. The *what might* is a major *what if.* The
systems of the FBI thrive on the *what if*, not allowing for multitudes of
Pandora's boxes outside the established pattern, in the gray of chaos.
The five-colored pattern of the Homeland Security Alert System stands
in testament. I'm supposed to believe that detecting patterns may make
the difference in thwarting the next terrorist attack. But I watched
government prosecutors chokehold and pin a guy who wasn't smart
enough to stand up for his chaos. Somehow, the fight isn't fair. I would
want to ask Ken Olsen, *if the fight wasn't fair why didn't you object?*

Sometimes, I roll my castor bean between my fingers. The little
thing is like Pandora's box. Open it and you get the promise of continual and escalating trouble. But the Pandora's box story also speaks
of hope in the bottom of the box. So, the castor bean isn't like it at all.
The more I roll it in my hand, infatuated, the more the shiny shell flakes
off. Underneath, it's gray as bars and locks.

Stronghold

The *Oxford English Dictionary* (*OED*) lists over fifty definitions of *hold*. There are explanations of *hold* as a noun (a firm hold), a verb (hold the cat), a phrasal verb (hold on to yourself), and an idiom (hold the phone, hold sway, hold water). *Hold's* compounds earn their own definitions: holdall, holdback, holdfast, holdout, holdover, holdup. The word was prolific in Old English. Scholars note in the *OED* that *hold* is one of the few words that appear consistently in the earliest known examples of writing, as far back as linguists can trace. Its spellings over the centuries have encompassed all the vowel combinations. Hold is "heold" is "hiad" is "hueld." The *OED* compilers prattle on as to whether *hold* "covers the same conceptual grounds as *keep*" and whether we should admit that *hold* is a synonym for *have*. *Hold* is the root of the name of the original angsty teen, Holden Caulfield, and as a musical symbol it is the Italian fermata, an arc and a dot over the note, sustained as long as the performer desires.

To have and keep in one's grasp

My mom's uncle, William Arthur Vogely, was born without lower legs. His body stumped at his thighs. From his left shoulder hung one slightly misshapen but still useful arm with hand, minus full fingers. From his right shoulder, nothing. Fine black hair charcoaled his skin. There was no explanation. He was a quarter century earlier than the thalidomide babies. His mother held him anyway. As long as she held him, so swaddled, no one would know what wasn't there.

He went to college but couldn't go to war. By this time he'd shed the fur. In fact, he was balding. During the war, he sat absolutely still and wrote intelligent letters to his brother, my grandpa, while Grandpa used his fully formed appendages to duck trench-grazing bullets. Grandpa wished he had not gone to war; it's not funny to say that Uncle Bill would have given an arm and a leg to go to war.

I met Uncle Bill when I was nineteen, at a staged and awkward family reunion at the Holiday Inn in Cape Girardeau, Missouri, blocks from the summer sloth of the Mississippi. The family hailed from everywhere *except* Missouri, but Grandpa's sister partook of oatmeal and bingo at the Cape Girardeau nursing home, and since she was the matriarch of the family by virtue of age, we descended with duty. (She wedded no husband and bore no children, so "she might be a lesbian," my mother whispered.) A wheelchair held her fragility. She perked up to wheel with Uncle Bill, whose robustness shamed the legged.

At our moment of meeting, Uncle Bill substituted a nod for a handshake. I don't remember what we talked about. His smile suggested he was friendly, personable, delighted to meet a distant niece from Ohio. I remember looking and not looking, noticing but not noticing, freaking and not freaking. He wasn't deformed. He was unformed. *I wonder if his wife carries him from wheelchair to toilet to tub to bed, and from bed to toilet to tub to wheelchair*. All his life held and carried, when he could not hold or carry, not his wife, not his two children, fully formed. He held knowledge in the form of a doctorate in mineral science from Princeton; in royalty checks from his thirty-three mineralogy textbooks; in professor emeritus status.

Later, I walked to the Mississippi and stared at the towering flood-wall breached a year earlier in the near-biblical floods of 1993. I couldn't picture the flood cresting. I couldn't picture the riverbanks and Army Corps of Engineers' floodwalls not doing their task, not holding the width of the river. The river defined width; the wall defined height. How ever did one definition overwhelm the other? For the rest of the reunion, I couldn't think of one worthwhile comment to contribute. I sat at the edge of things. I should have been more mature.

I have this memory of being told that Uncle Bill died five years later, following a doctor's exam gone wrong. On the way from wheelchair to exam table in the oncology ward, a nurse dropped him. *She dropped him.* Could not hold him, could not hold on when all anyone had ever done for this man was to make sure something held him. His fall cracked a hip and he succumbed a few weeks later from a combination of everything. I imagine he had a full-length coffin only because I doubt half-length coffins exist, and that in death as in the moment of infancy, family did not have to face his deformity. His obituary made no mention of his deformity, and maybe that was right and maybe it was wrong. There is no section headlined "Obituaries of the Deformed" because the sum of ourselves is not figured by what we never had. In the end is this beginning: Love defined was the birth-weary mother not even questioning what to do with the wet halfling on the sheet. She held him.

To have in recognition of achievement

On the other side of my family, via my father's lineage, the shine of old glasshouses radiate. Horticultural rites of passage marked my growth. My first tomato plant, my first transplanted herb, my first mistake with a cactus. I learned to count by inventorying the tropical foliage. I perfected penmanship and spelling by scripting signs with markers and cardboard for houseplants, vegetables, and fertilizer. I was the only eight-year-old on the planet who knew that the correct spelling of poinsettia included no "*t*" in the middle and an "*i*" near the end. "*Point-set-ta,*" said the customers. "*Poin-set-tia,*" I corrected from my perch by the cash register. "*Isn't she darling,*" they said.

I decided I would be a grownup for real when I could carry as many plants as my father. Shifting inventory and seasonal sales meant he was always relocating plants from one greenhouse to another. Our plants moved like nomadic tribes. The medium-sized houseplants in plastic pots presented the best opportunities for plant-carrying prowess. Dad would cluster three plants, then take hold of the pot rims from above, right where the three pots touched. With this method, he could hold three plants, sometimes four, per hand and sometimes scoop a couple into the crook of his arm and chest. Eight plants at a time! No broken leaves! A new greenhouse record (if not an outright world record) for Most Plants Carried with Bare Hands!

I could not wait for adult hands so I could hold plants the way my dad held orchids and ferns. It never occurred to me that as a woman, my hands would never be as big, nor as strong. Their slimness I do not regret. I have always been able to hold what's necessary.

I once got a promotion because I knew how to carry many plants at one time. The year was 2001.The place was a wholesale greenhouse in Ames, Iowa. The season was the mad rush of May. I had earned my master's degree and taught for a year but was burned out on writing and literature, desperate to do the one other thing I excelled at, greenhouse work, while my boyfriend finished his own degree.

The second-generation owner, a man with an enormous gut and a quick temper, hired me with caution. "If you like greenhouses so much, why aren't you working with your family?"

Caught unprepared, I shrugged and looked away, at the black and white photos decorating the office. They could have very well hung from the walls in Hirt's Greenhouse. They showed the owner's father watering, potting, proud as petals regarding his sun-drenched greenhouse. *Because it's not so different here.* He shuffled my application papers and asked if I could start on Monday.

In this wholesale greenhouse, plants started from seeds or cuttings, then were sold to retailers. Twelve Quonset-style greenhouses covered thousands of trays of perennials and annuals. The trays were called flats and each flat held twelve three-packs, making thirty-six perennial sproutlings per flat. My task was to help fill orders for flats. A retail

An employee, Sam Brown, in the main greenhouse sometime in the 1940s

garden store might order ten flats of white impatiens, fifteen of marigolds, and three of each shade of petunia. I would help carry the flats from the Quonsets to the delivery truck. The job was going to be mindless and wonderful. I could get dirty and relish the ache of muscles that, for the last two years, hadn't held more than a pen, a book bag, and a strong drink.

On my first afternoon I met Brett, a long-time employee. He drove a truck whose back window doubled as a shrine to Dale Earnhardt. Brett had stenciled "DALE I MISS YOU" below racing stickers. Brett manned the order form, a clipboard, and a walkie-talkie, tools of the order-fillers. The walkie-talkie was for staying in contact with the other order-filling crews, because knowledge of a couple hundred flowers spread across twelve houses required numerous minds. His crew included two high school boys and me. He snapped his fingers and we dutifully followed him through the Quonsets. When he handed me two flats of coleus, I requested two more. He said "*You sure?*" I nodded. Long ago I'd learned to balance extra flats on my arms, the way a waitress holds plates in the slight bend of her elbow. Brett shrugged and snipped at the boys for not carrying more. Later, when Brett couldn't find the salvia and I spotted their leafy stalks from the far end of the Quonset, he stared at me.

The next morning, Brett held an extra walkie-talkie, clipboard, and order form. He bestowed them upon me and pointed at two high school boys kicking gravel. He tapped the order form. "We need this one filled in an hour. Call if you can't find something. Don't fuck up. The boss is in a mood today."

To aim or direct

A boy I'll call Josh was my brother's friend, and Josh lived next to a jungled lot whose rotting center was a soft-spined farmhouse, condemned. Josh was the junior class president at Buckeye Senior High, a typical position at a typical school. He achieved status not through politics and public speaking, but with popularity and a diamond smile. With such ranking, Josh had no problem gathering groups for nighttime treks to the dark-windowed house. Insert *haunted* as necessary. My brother, Matt, sometimes heeled behind Josh. *Sometimes* matters, because Matt was not there the night Josh, rural tour guide promising pee-your-pants good times, swung open the farmhouse door to the glint of a rifle. My brother was not in the line of teens who saw Josh collapse at the instant the man aiming the rifle knocked a slug through Josh's jugular collared by curly hair the girls loved. Nothing held Josh's blood.

The rifleman did not, does not, will not, understand the ramifications. He reasoned that since the trespassers outnumbered him, he had a right to defend his property, his stronghold. Parents perched *murder* on their lips. A jury held him accountable. *Hold* morphs from verb to noun. His prison cell is a hold.

I construct the scenario from a single conversation with my parents and my skimming of the *Medina County Gazette* as it bannered the details. I have never questioned my brother about the murder. I always assumed that since he didn't talk about it he wasn't there. Of all the perspectives unspoken from that night, this one is most silent. What if Matt *was* there?

If so, a tangle of possibilities knots the tidy narrative. He lagged behind the group. He stopped to smoke at the edge of the field. He dared Josh to go first. He forgot his flashlight and returned to his truck. He opened a different door. Or through a window he saw the rifleman, deduced what was about to happen, and ran.

I would understand if he convinced himself he wasn't there, wasn't a witness. Novelist Charles Baxter says, "strategic amnesia has everything to do with the desire to create or destroy personal histories." The strategic amnesia may be mine, may be Matt's, may be ours. If he was there but somehow left the scene before the authorities arrived, the power of denial and the fear of complicity would have counseled him to stay quiet. His strategic amnesia would have been deep and protective, destroying a history. My strategic amnesia created the only safe narrative of the night.

A gun shifts from safe to dangerous depending on who's holding it. I can say the same for this memory from 1993. I don't remember Matt's mood in the aftermath. Could I ask him now, catch him on his cell phone and toss the question? Ruin his day for what memories he holds?

To keep from falling

Anthropologists have noted that standing upright spurs negative side effects. Our vital organs hang like bull's-eyes on the dartboards of our chests; our weight distribution eventually compresses our spines; our arches fall, our joints ache, our holes redden with hemorrhoids since thin tissues cannot resist such gravity. So why do we stand? There are theories, and here's my favorite, culled from an anthropology text.

Picture female primates and their infants in a diorama of the dawn of modern humans. Most primates walked on all fours. However, females with infants walked on threes. One hand held the infant, cupped against chest and belly as the mother tricycled away from danger. When the infant was strong enough, the mother would hoist it onto her back where, it was assumed, the little primate would hold tight while the mother loped to safety.

But there was a problem. The little ones often fell. Perhaps a female chimp who had lost one too many babes to the jaguar tried a different approach. When danger crinkled leaves in the thicket, she ran as usual, but the infant was not on her back, not cradled in one black hand. She held Baby tight in *both* hands. Two appendages for holding, two for running. She escaped. Her offspring, keepers of the genetic behavior for holding with two hands, survived. Generations shifted from holding the young with one arm to holding with both, simultaneously learning to stand upright in order to hold. Safer infants meant more infants matured. The ones that matured were the ones held, the ones holding the new genes for the new behavior. It was simple survival of the species, a species holding on.

To keep from departing or getting away

As a child, I asked God to grant me the power to read minds, and when that failed I asked him to make someone realize I was gifted and should be promptly enrolled in a special school, and when that failed I taught myself to catch chameleons in the dank corners of greenhouses. Chameleons in Ohio! They arrived on palms bagged in brown sleeves. The Greeks called them ground lions. I called them something I needed to hold.

Sitting cross-legged, I pressed my calves against the cement floor and watched the long row of ivy, waiting for a sequential flicker of leaves that would mean a tiny lizard lion was fording stem and vine. I'd step softly in my red 'Roo shoes with the zipper pocket and white laces. If the prey was a ground lion, then my hands were the sky lions, doming over, then under, the chameleon. Cupped, I held cold-blood-dry-skin long-tail-blinkless-eyes. Dropped them in jars, loosed them on ledgers spread on Mom's desk, boasted their capture. At the end of the day I freed them. Theodore Roethke claimed in his journals that he was "done with every pretty thing" and to that I pin *liar*. I haven't caught a chameleon in two decades, but I might as well be catching them every day. This quandary of a secret I share now for the first time: When chameleons die, they come back as ivy. Every pretty thing in its right place.

Full understanding, as in holding knowledge

In 2001, Dad announced the Hirt family was Jewish. He'd learned this from the 1900 census, or maybe some naturalization papers, or

maybe a random document he found online. Dad had been researching
family trees as if they channeled a path straight to Elysium Fields. On
the paperwork, Great-Grandpa Sam scrawled the j-word in a box next
to his name. Dad said it meant "Jew," and he held the photocopy like a
chalice. He smacked it down in front of osteoporotic Grandma and
said, with smugness, "You lied to me." Grandma had always said the
Hirts were Austrian and German. *And Protestant, but none devout.*

"You didn't need to know that he was Jewish," she retorted, then
added, "If you look too hard you'll find something you shouldn't know."

Grandpa refused to comment, but he was senile and probably did
not understand. Dad claims his sister walked out when he revealed the
discovery, and that his brother stared blankly. His brother was married
to a stylish German woman who had retained her German citizenship
all the years she'd lived in Ohio. I heard all this in summary, via phone,
far away. I cringed.

When I was hardly off the phone with Dad, Mom called me with
"Advice on the Jewish Situation."

"You might not want to tell Paul," she said.

Paul was my boyfriend of five years. Already I was planning to narrate
this news to him, anticipating his incredulous reaction.

Mom mistook my silence as a request for further advice. "He might
leave you. Some people see Jews as, well, *lower.* There's a social stigma."

Mom's surfacing prejudice and Dad's enthusiasm fascinated me. I
asked my blond-haired, blue-eyed, six-foot-two brother what he thought
about Mom's prediction of social alienation, and he said, "Hey, I'm the
Aryan. What do I know?" He reported Dad was one day shy of wearing
a yarmulke.

Humor aside, the discovery meant a lot to my father. He'd grown
up in a cold, hands-off family. No one shared stories. No family photos
graced the walls. The only heirloom was the business. Hugging was for
holidays. Religious faith was nonexistent. Everyone was sedate and as
inoffensive as white bread. In response, Dad embraced the notion of a
secret Jew fathering a long line of businessmen. Why? Did he view
scandal as truth? Was it a ready-made identity? Was it the identity his
parents did not want him to have? Was it a clue, a Rosetta Stone?

Dad had long insisted there was a secret in the family. He cited the exile of distant Aunt Debbie. He noted that Grandma never spoke to Grandpa's brother. He researched the possibilities of half-truths regarding the World War I drowning of Paul Hirt, the merchant marine on the ill-fated *Otranto*. For years I pressed him for details about the secret. He circled it and never landed. None of his evidence linked to a larger picture. This newest discovery consumed his imagination. He hardly knew what was more scandalous, the original cover-up, or Grandma's planned perpetuation of the cover-up. Dad emailed every Hirt in the nation, revealing Sam Hirt's heritage, trying to locate other Jewish Hirts. One Hirt turned up in Pullman, Washington, eight miles from my apartment in Moscow, Idaho. *Go find out if he looks Jewish*, my dad emailed. I hit delete as fast as possible.

"Why bother?" I asked one afternoon, worried that my dad was upsetting the family (and pestering every Hirt in America) by spending so much time and effort clarifying a past that might not reveal anything. It was very obvious to me that political currents from the past century made lying about heritage and religion a decent defensive maneuver. I wasn't privy to the larger picture Dad held in his head, unable to articulate to me.

"I have to find out who I am." For a long time, that's all he could give me.

I pointed out he was more than his ancestors, more than their deceits.

Dad didn't start his genealogy hobby until he learned I was writing essays exploring Hirt's Greenhouse. He likes to point out that my version of family history is "unusual" and not what he recalls. Mom takes that stance too—to this day she claims no memory of that odd phone call about the Jewish situation. For awhile, Dad phoned me the moment he confirmed a new bit of information about a dead relative. On holiday visits he piled stacks of poorly copied pages in front of me—the census, court rulings, rambling emails from other people named Hirt. Evidence. Of what? My memory research has triggered his quest for official documents, documents he studies in order to construct his own memory of the family.

To be filled by, contain

In elementary school, a top shelf at the library held blue-bound books about famous Americans. I feared boredom moldered in their heavy pages, and I was already unimpressed with famous Americans, so I never read the blue top shelf. But I knew volume six championed Helen Keller, blind and deaf and an example to us all.

I never understood how she communicated, how she knew she was human in a world of humans. Twenty years later, I read her autobiography and learned. With no sight and no sound, she was left with taste, touch, and smell. Her tutor took touch and transformed language like this: She put an object, a small pillow, say, in Helen's hand. In the other hand, the tutor drew letters. The stick and curve of the p, the dot of the i, the long beds of double l. Letters appeared on Helen's skin and sunk like little fish into her blood, schooling in her brain to arrange the p, the i, the l's, the owl of o and the silent snowcapped w. Pillow. A pillow in each hand. She held the words to read them.

Letters became a feeling. They were their curves, their spaces, their singular flat existence on her skin. Other than for a few brief years, she never knew words as sounds or as black curls on white paper. She only knew them as feelings. I should omit *only*. She knew them as feelings. There's nothing *only* about that.

If you were Helen's teacher, you'd have to write this entire essay in her hand, to give it to her to hold and understand. If skin were paper, what would your body reveal to you? What would you spell on the shoulders of the boy you loved in high school; what would you ask on the neck of the girl you fancied since third grade? Remember Jung: "The creative mind plays with the objects it loves." I think, deep down, I cannot help but envy Helen Keller's chance to skip words as sounds, as objects of sight, to hold them in sequence on palm upturned.

Not so simple are the holdings of memory, nor the meanings held in words. A primate holds her infant two-handed and a species thrives. At another time and place, two human hands hold a rifle, and two more slip nervously off the skin of old Uncle Bill, so two die. I know Helen Keller could not have understood every sentence lettered into her palm. Letters slipped, words blurred.

Yet in her attempts she was the supreme musician, transforming the fermata. Cue and hold. Anticipate the resonance. When writing I type, as if letters rain from my fingertips to become footprints, words on a screen. What I've held I'm letting go. These words are the chameleons I've kept close to my surname, the ground lions set loose like secrets in a stronghold where I am both defender and trespasser.

Laying Dynamite with the Ninth Duke of Devonshire

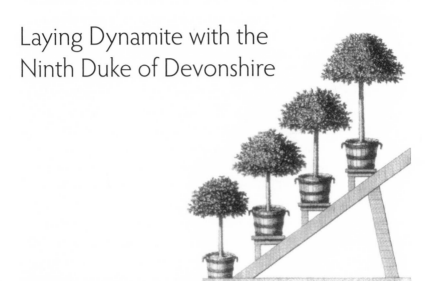

Not being able to go back to my greenhouses is a strange feeling. I go back to the space, to the corner of land, and I stare at the CVS pharmacy. It's stupid, corporate, built exactly like every other CVS. Each year, it becomes harder for me to remember how the greenhouses sat on the land. It always occurs to me that I could pass the place by, not stop at all. My grandparents are buried just down the road. Why not visit their graves? I never do. I just sit in the CVS parking lot and stare and don't know why.

If I could revisit the past, though, I wouldn't go back to my greenhouses.

I would without hesitation request an invite to the Great Conservatory of Chatsworth, England, in December of 1843. That winter, Queen Victoria and Prince Albert rode in a horse-drawn carriage down the center aisle of the largest greenhouse in the world. She was twenty-four, already six years into her sixty-three-year reign; Albert (her cousin) had been her husband for three years. They visited the glass structure at night because they could. The incandescent lamp had been invented a few years earlier, and while Edison's light bulb was still thirty-six years in the future, the short-lived Victorian lamps were a novelty fit for royalty. A stunning twelve thousand lamps hung from the iron ribs of the greenhouse, courtesy of Joseph Paxton, builder and gardener of the Great Conservatory. And it's Joseph Paxton whom I want to meet. Like the poet Roethke, Paxton is an ancestor in my horticulture bloodline.

I know how worthwhile the visit must have been for queen and prince, seeing light twinkling off the glass and arches inspired by cathedrals. But Paxton had visions beyond the fancies of architecture, for he knew the incandescents were only meant to showcase the phenomenal collection of exotics he tended for the owner of Chatsworth, the sixth Duke of Devonshire. The Great Conservatory at Chatsworth, completed in 1841 after five years of construction, was renowned not only for its size and defiance of all known architectural guidelines, but also for what it housed, plants foreign to gray old England. Plants fanciful, strange, beautiful and terrifying. Paxton was the only one who could grow them. The duke so admired Paxton's prowess that he said of the horticultural prodigy, *I had rather all the plants were dead than have you ill.*

On the night of the queen's visit, I picture this. As the carriage pony's hooves tocked the stone floor, Paxton and the duke stepped alongside, excited tour guides in their jungle. Here was the Walton Date Palm, nearly full-grown with room to spare in the sixty-seven-foot heights of the Great Conservatory. They hoped it would bear sweet dark dates, a hope not unfounded, since Paxton had coaxed fruit from a peculiar dwarf banana tree. Next were hibiscus flowers with wide blossoms never before attained in captivity. Then the rare *erythrina arborea,* the short coral tree with red flowers, shadowed by *cocos plumosa,* an actual coconut tree thriving under glass in the center of gloomy England. Pink bougainvillea cascaded on thorny vines. Bulbs bloomed under an orange tree. And from every angle, deep into the curved recesses grayed by four miles worth of steam pipes for heating, leaves and vines and stems of types inconceivable and strange displayed themselves for the queen and the prince.

The duke's centerpiece in the greenhouse was *dracaena draco*, the dragon tree, a specimen doubled in worth because it was also a gift from one Lord Fitzwilliam. In the Victorian Era, the gift of an exotic plant rivaled jewels and fine wine. The story of the dragon tree is so rich I'm sure that Paxton, who was brilliant, halted the pony and spread his arms wide to introduce the woody, funnel-shaped tree with its dense branches uplifted at uniform angles. Leaves like sword blades crowned the top. The queen and the prince would have said they'd never seen anything like it, and Paxton, ever the showman, would have stepped under its shadow to swipe a pocket knife against a thin branch. He would have warned the young queen she was about to see something unsettling. She hardly flinched, I'm sure, but maybe the pony sidestepped in its harness and snorted. Paxton would have held the cut branch in his palm, and a crimson liquid would have pooled against his white skin. Dragon blood. Legend spoke of the first *dracaena draco*, rooting from the corpse of Pau Tangula, the mythic sea dragon of the Solomon Islands. All the descendants of that tree carried the blood of dragons. Would Paxton have added that natives of the Canary Islands, where Europeans had first seen the dragon tree a century before, believed that since the venerable trees bled, they also had souls? Or that unscrupulous goldseekers cut countless dragon trees, letting their red sap harden into balls of "dragon fruit," sold in underground markets as aphrodisiacs? Maybe he dropped the witchcraft and myth-mongering for an ending that appealed to the refined artistic temperament of his guests. He would have explained how the red resin of *dracaena draco* was prized by Italian violinmakers mixing varnishes for their instruments.

Had I sat in the carriage with the queen and the prince, listening to dark-eyed Paxton (and no doubt developing a crush on him and his greenhouse), I would have wondered if the dragon tree harbored more than a soul. I would have wagered it knew the color of sound. Years later, Queen Victoria knighted Paxton for his achievements. I think he's an avatar. When I sit at the CVS and stare at what is and isn't there, maybe I'm waiting for a story as fine as the dragon tree myth, or a neo-Victorian as divine as Paxton, something or someone to bring me meaning, to make the space matter again.

The Duke of Devonshire, with his wealth and connections, and Joseph Paxton, garden boy with an unflagging sense of vision and accomplishment, were a duo who refined the British horticultural world. Praise abounds. More than I wish to praise them, I wish to tell them I once had a plant they would have set on a pedestal in the Great Conservatory for Queen Victoria's viewing.

When my boyfriend, Paul, and I lived in Ames, Iowa, our neighbors in apartment no. 5 fought like wildcats. Paul finally called 911 in response to their post-midnight *go to hells* and their penchant for whipping furniture against the walls, denting space with expletives. They were always kicking each other out. Even though their actions seemingly verged on murder, I can forgive them their domestic disputes. They were young and Midwest poor, unhappy, strung out. But I cannot forgive them for leaving an old philodendron on their front step on a February night, the watery cells of its elephantine leaves freezing to death. Forgiveness I deny them because I live by one maxim, inspired by my connection to my family's greenhouse—take care of the plants. Neglect was not acceptable. Joseph Paxton knows what I mean.

I noticed the plant on the front steps as I headed to the store. This variety of philodendron I had not seen often, a spherical trunk tapered up into a prodigious spray of stems, sleek and green as leeks. From each stem's end hung one tremendous leaf, a foot long and foot wide, a leaf spawned from a surrealist oak and a nuclear winter oak. Crusty aerial roots stretched from the stems and jutted from the trunk, thick and obscene in their quest for soil. It was the most magnificent philodendron I'd ever seen outside of a greenhouse. I registered a newfound dislike of my short-tempered neighbors, now that they had kicked out a plant, the one living thing in their apartment unable to retaliate.

I could only wonder at its trespass. Had it grown too big? Did it get in the way of the TV? Did it smell funky? Was it tossed because it had no flowers? Was it the latest victim of their domestic disputes? Maybe the boyfriend had failed to kick out the girlfriend, or vice versa, and revenge meant ousting the offender's plant. Or I could give them the benefit of the doubt. Maybe the neighbors were cleaning. Maybe the plant had bugs. Maybe an impending move made the plant expendable.

I promised myself to take in the plant if it was still out in the cold when I returned.

It was. I did.

In the twenty minutes I'd spent buying chips and beer, the philodendron had deflated into a limp bouquet on its way to freezing solid, like celery in an icebox. I hefted its fifty pounds down the stairs to my basement apartment. I set it in the bathtub, turned on the hot water, closed the door, and started steam therapy. Paul stood in the hallway and asked what I was doing. What thing had I hauled in? I said that if I could cease the freezing of the trunk, I could save the plant. He said, "What?" and opened the door. I closed it and said, "Don't." He said, "You're being creepy." I filled the tub halfway, so that scalding water lapped against the tall white pot. I examined the big old leaves and deemed them goners. With red scissors I cut all save one, leaving stubs of stem and a tiny leaf. From the soil surface, where a lattice of aerial roots had sunk their probing tips, I extracted cigarette butts and a handful of broken yellow pencils.

I had respect for this veteran philodendron. The mature trunk intrigued me. It was ringed like a coconut palm, but spotted with a pattern of almond circles that once were the base of stems. Someone had shaped it, coning the trunk and cutting stems until it was more like a sculpture than a wild philodendron. I placed its age at twenty years, maybe thirty, based on the width of the trunk. An old houseplant is rare. How had my undeserving neighbors come to own this specimen? The plant couldn't have been in their care for their entire lives.

I tended it for two hours, emptying the fifty-four gallon hot water tank as I tried to maintain the steam, irritating Paul, who had to forgo his shower. I knew any respectable greenhouse worker would laugh at my desperate attempt at resuscitation. When tropical plants freeze, they die. Horticulture 101 would propose this solution: Throw it away. I wasn't willing. If I had nabbed the philodendron in time, I had done so with literally minutes to spare. Those minutes meant something, even though I knew I should have grabbed it the moment I saw it. I did not really know if the plant would survive, if mere humidity could halt the crystal of frost. Steam was my apology and my promise.

When the trunk felt warm and the top layer of soil evanesced that familiar peaty scent, I moved the plant to a crate by the window. Clear sap dripped from the amputated stems, a good sign, for at least the sap could flow. *At least I don't bring home stray animals,* I told Paul when he pointed out that the trimmed plant took up a significant square of space, so it was sure to fill half the living room when it rebounded, and wasn't that problematic in our small apartment? *Think of all the oxygen it will emit,* I responded.

The plant basked in morning and afternoon sun. I dosed it with fertilizer. I sat with it every night, just looking and thinking. Comforting the plant felt good, lucid, relaxed. I sipped wine and knew the philodendron wasn't dead because I could imagine new leaves that would arch from the strange trunk, how tender aerial roots would straggle and harden before nudging soil. I also understood injured plants reproduce wildly to compensate for a lost limb or a torn leaf or a sheared root. Certainly the continual injury of living with my neighbors had spurred the plant to its formidable size. After two weeks, defying the February cold, the plant sprouted stems whose tips unfurled like scrolls. At the library, I scanned horticulture books and found I owned a *philodendron selloum,* the tree philodendron. Within a month, massive leaves cast shadows across my bookshelves. I decided that while I had been sitting there looking at the philodendron, it had been considering my books.

If that philodrendron could have read anything, it would have read about Yggdrasill, the "world tree" of Norse mythology. Yggdrasill makes the tree in the Garden of Eden look like a particle board stage prop.

Yggdrasill is the universe dressed up as a tree. Yggdrasill's roots grip soil in the underworld. A standard tree trunk rises from this pit, branching into a trinity. The south stem's branches shelter the past, the present, and the future. The north stem's branches are home to the frost giant, Mimir, and his fountain of wisdom. The center branch skewers the orb of earth, breaking through Asgard Mountain and leafing out into Valhalla, the heaven of the Norse gods. From below, the leaves are clouds and the fruits are stars. A zoo of animals lives in Yggdrassil, and some are mischievous. The serpent, Nidhoggr, fangs the roots, for he dreams of the world ending in a hiss. Too far away to see the wrongdoings of Nidhoggr sits a nameless eagle, protector of the air. The squirrel, Batatosk, runs up and down the trunk all day, trying to pit the serpent and the eagle in a death match, but no one listens to him. Meanwhile, four stags live in the branches. Their names are noble: Dain, Dvalin, Duneyr, and Durathor. At dawn, dew gathers on their antlers. When they rise to graze the leaves, dew drips to earth as rain.

My tree philodendron could have been Yggdrasill. Its roots sank deep into the core of a pot. I could not twist them free. The strange trunk was perfect for Batatosk's fast feet, his worry-tail twirling. Mimir, the giant from the north stem, helped it survive the frost of February. And the plant sprouted leaves shaped like the racks of stags, leaves that dripped water like the staghorns dripped dew.

Amusingly, scholars have devoted significant research to identify Yggdrasill. One popular opinion classifies the tree as some sort of evergreen, not necessarily a pine tree, but literally a forever-green tree, eternal and immune to seasonal variations. The other notion, for the hardliners, categorizes Yggdrasill as an ash tree, because Norse legend holds the first human sprang from an ash tree. I say, *Who cares what the hell kind of tree it is? Isn't anyone concerned about the squirrel, young Batatosk? All day, up and down that tree.* I want to play with Batatosk because he is consumed with worry. I want to tell him the eagle will never listen, and the serpent will never cease, because I too have been tearing paths between demise and redemption, to no fruitful end. I want to show him the deer in the leaves because he cannot conceive of them, yet he must.

And I want him to help me. I want him to tell me how to get out of my parking lot, to stop my pointless pilgrimage. Maybe I want him to tell me that the eagle does listen.

In the movie *Harold and Maude*, teenage introvert Harold falls in love with free-spirited Maude, a woman old enough to be his grandmother. A series of scenes juxtaposing their freakish pastimes (strangers' funerals, demolitions) ends with Maude doting over tiny plants in a greenhouse. The place is expansive, bigger, I realize immediately, than my greenhouses. The tiny plants, nestled in terra cotta pots, stretch to the

My grandmother, Onalee Hirt, outside the North House

edge of the frame. Harold stands two rows over, so tense that his shoulders brush his earlobes.

"I like to watch things grow," says Maude, each word a smile and a psalm.

Later, Maude steals a sickly city tree and speeds it to the forest, where she and Harold solemnly replant it in a grove of giants, where it will grow unhindered by concrete and smog. Where Maude acts on her ability to listen to plants, I see myself far too often. Such delightful disobedience. Such horticultural heroics. I too want to save the doomed.

Paxton, meanwhile, never dealt in half-dead trees. The duke, in his zeal for collecting exotics, was often sending Paxton to procure plants that were absurdly vivacious. The duke once bought a mature palm tree from Lady Tankerville, who was so rich she owned a private palm greenhouse. The palm weighed twelve tons, and the trunk was eight feet around. The duke deemed it perfect for the Great Conservatory. He and Paxton hired workers to dismantle Lady Tankerville's palm house frame by frame, girder by girder, because there was no other way to get the palm out. Then the workers dug (somehow), and transported the tree along the roads, probably with less turmoil than Maude's tree-stealing caper. For the palm to pass, authorities dismantled the turnpikes between Surrey and Devonshire. Lucky for the duke and Paxton, the Great Conservatory was not totally finished. The five hundred workers they employed helped angle the palm inside and finished the greenhouse around it. The duke's and Paxton's obsession makes me bet Maude would have turned down young Harold for a date with the Victorian era gentlemen.

Paxton was so protective of the Great Conservatory that he refused to let most visitors inside. He made them peer through the glass. Paxton, however, had to relent when his *Victoria regia* water lily bloomed. Word spread when lily pads strong enough to hold little girls not only grew, but thrived so wildly that they blossomed white flowers fragrant as pineapples.

If any event set the stage for the Victorian Era's reputation as the age of imitation, it was Paxton's success with this humongous, finicky water lily native to the South American backwaters of the Amazon. When European explorers sighted the six-foot wide lily pads near Guiana and Bolivia, their first thought was to offer the fantastic plants as gifts to royalty, a trend all the rage back in the homeland. The edges of the leaves bent up at uniform right angles, making the lilies appear to be shallow bowls. The undersides were red. The white lotus-like flowers were extraordinary, the flowers of fairy tales.

The problem, encountered by numerous botanists over the first half of the nineteenth century, was one of transport. Six-foot water lilies bearing fifteen-inch flowers presented logistical challenges rarely encountered by the botanists and their little trowels and tidy pots of orchids and young ferns. Thaddeus Haenke tried in 1801, and botanical lore holds that he secured viable seeds, but he died mysteriously in 1817 and his entire collection was lost. Alcide d'Orbigny pickled the seeds before shipping them to Paris. He also sent a leaf. By the time the items arrived, most certainly ragged from travel, the recipients weren't even sure what they were getting. The seeds molded. Someone folded the giant leaf to store it, an action so careless it later prompted British botanists to scoff at French botanists. Folding the giant water lily! How criminal!

Robert Schomburk, in 1831, was the first European to actually take an intact water lily leaf across the Atlantic, arriving in London where the botanist John Lindley met him at the port and was able to examine the rotting remains, confidently naming it a new genus of plant. It was he who christened it *Victoria regia,* in honor of the queen.

Fourteen years later, Thomas Bridges, a tourist, succeeded where the botanists failed. While hunting in Bolivia, he found the lilies in a placid turn of the Amazon River. He preserved flower buds in bottles of liquor. He packed twenty-two seeds into cubes of clay. Twenty rotted by the time he docked in London. Two sprouted under the nervous hands of gardeners at the royal Kew Gardens. Success, however, remained in the shadows of the Amazon. The Kew specimens grew, barely. No lily flowers graced the limp pads with their pale undersides.

In the summer of 1849, when Paxton viewed the lilies at Kew, he deduced the problem immediately. The lilies were set in stagnant pools of unmoving water. Their native Amazon was a river, not a lake. Back at the Great Conservatory, Paxton built a pool with a water wheel. The wheel circulated the water, making currents. Paxton was a true Victorian. His cleverness in imitation was unsurpassed. The gardeners at Kew sent him one languishing five-leaf lily, each lily pad all of six inches wide, on a special train that made no stops. By September, the lily pads were forty inches wide; by October, fifty inches. On November 2, 1849, Paxton announced that he saw a flower bud which looked "like a large peach placed in a cup. No words can describe the grandeur." Seven days later, at dusk, the *Victoria regia* bloomed. The flower remained open for thirty-six hours. The gardeners from Kew heeded Paxton's urgent message to come immediately, to witness the sight "worth a journey of a thousand miles." Queen Victoria visited, too. Over the next year, the lily gave 112 blossoms. Paxton built a special greenhouse for the lily, with a larger pool and adequate aisles for viewing by the curious public.

When I moved to Idaho, I gave my philodendron to a friend who was staying in Iowa. With its long stems and wide leaves, it needed almost twelve cubic feet of space. I didn't dare cram it into the dark of the moving truck for a four-day trip, its plant cells atrophying every minute past the usual dark of night, the furniture and boxes shifting to crinkle leaves and snap stems. I would have made a terrible botanical explorer. Yet when I arrived at my Idaho apartment after half a week on the road, the thin leaves of an unwanted houseplant poked from the dumpster. I lifted it out and smiled. I had no idea what it was, but it was mine. Days later I visited a florist's shop in town and bought a new philodendron, not a tree species, but a split-leaf species. No staghorn leaves here. The foliage spread into shapes like breastplates and hearts and ribs and dragonheads. I was happy. New plants, new home.

Joseph Paxton died in 1865. A succession of dukes owned the Chatsworth estate at Devonshire, but it never again achieved the grandeur it had in the 1840s, with lilies and queens and incandescent lamps like soft stars. World War I drained the life from the Great Conservatory. Coal for heating was scarce and the tropical exotics died slowly. The ranks of gardeners who tended the structure turned plowshares to swords. By 1918, there was literally no one left to water the palms or replant the hibiscus or bed the bulbs for springtime flowers. Eight million soldiers, and every plant in the Great Conservatory at Chatsworth, died in the four years of war. In 1920, distressed by the rundown conservatory and haunted by all it could no longer represent, the ninth Duke of Devonshire purchased dynamite. Some accounts claim he was accompanied by Paxton's grandson. They set bundles at the corroded bases of the arched girders. They lit fuses that twisted like the hisses of serpents in the wildest Norse dreams of Nidhoggr. The great structure shuddered at the explosions, but it did not fall. The duke and the grandson tried again. And again. After six tremendous explosions, the Great Conservatory reluctantly collapsed on itself.

It is easy to say I wish I had been at the Great Conservatory when the queen and the prince first visited, that spectacular night before a world war, when incandescent lamps were strange new things, when the simple presence of exotic plants was a privilege. That is the easy wish

One of the 1940 greenhouses, now empty, winter 2003

indeed. It is the wish for timelessness and success, as if nothing else is
worthy. But the wish is picture-book idealistic, as fanciful as Yggdrasill,
the mythic, eternal tree, despite the serpent gnawing the roots.

How much more difficult to place myself in 1920, laying dynamite
with the ninth duke and the grandson who would not inherit all his
grandfather had built. I can't do it, just like I can't get a single thought
through my head when I sit and stare at the CVS. I think I can imagine

my brother in 1920. He would have understood why the duke sought to bring down the ruin, to ease its cracking ribs, to calm its panic over empty space. There is something to be said for the person who can bring down what's falling anyway, yet can still escape from beneath it.

I am reminded of a night in October 2006, a year and four months after the greenhouses were demolished. I'm in town for the weekend, staying at my brother's house in Medina. In his backyard sits Hirt's Gardens—two new greenhouses bookending a small garden store, with a few hoop houses stretching behind it all. The new name is a combination of what the business used to be. Under my grandparents' ownership, it was (for a time) Strongsville Gardens. My parents and uncle ran it as Hirt's Greenhouse. Now, with all the generations funneled into the last male descendant, Hirt's Gardens is born.

Everything in the greenhouses is sold online through a website and Ebay auctions. It's a way of business that Sam and Anna and Hobart and Onalee could not have imagined; my brother can't imagine anything else. Over the next few years, I will see signs of unrivaled online success. Matt and Dad will build more greenhouses and get their own semi-private mailman who arrives with an empty truck just to pick up their packages. They have nice computers, new cars, an ATV with a snowplow. They pave the drive, erect a fence, and install security systems. They hire employee after employee just to help fill internet orders, day after day.

My brother takes me through his house. Built decades ago by a paranoid survivalist, the house features a bunker/panic room in the basement. A massive steel door opens into a wood-lined room full of cabinets, racks, and small cupboards. "For his guns," says Matt, "his ammunition." The room is amazing, the former owner a mystery. My brother has no idea what to do with the room. He just shows it to visitors, leaves it empty, contemplates the strange steel door and all it was meant to keep out in the moment of the last stand, Armageddon, bitter ends.

We head upstairs. The greenhouses glow in his backyard, surrounded by darkness not so different from the darkness in that 1943 photo of the original greenhouses. I feel like I'm on the moon, looking back at the earth.

In the living room, Matt smokes cigarettes and watches St. Louis win the World Series. He's smoked forever, but this is the first time I've seen him do it. I feel grownup.

I flip through a gigantic binder of color photos of plants and the greenhouses. He has taken hundreds of images. A few show a magnificent dragonfly up close, its translucent wings caught in perfect focus. Matt tells me that the military has been trying to mimic dragonfly flight for years now; they can't get it right. He says it with pride, as if his photo has ascertained the secret of the wings. I continue through the album, and he remembers taking each picture—when he took it, why, what caught his eye, how many times he had to retake it to get it right. The albums are sweet. For so many years I saw my little brother as a slacker, always in trouble, barely passing high school. I regret misjudging him. I'm fascinated he has an interest, and he's good at it, and he, like me, has found his own way to document the greenhouses. When the Series ends, he promptly heads to bed, telling me there's a Dunkin' Donuts down the street, for breakfast. I put away the album and bed down on a mattress on the floor. I notice that the vinyl blinds are a brittle dirty yellow from cigarette smoke.

The next morning, in the greenhouses, he walks me down every aisle, and his commentary has a theme: danger. First, we view the gloriosa lilies, which Matt claims are coveted in the terrorist training camps because they are poisonous. Second, the poppies, cousins of the heroin poppies blooming in Afghanistan. Third, the carnivorous plants, their sticky leaves tricking flies and aphids into a slow death, a gradual dissolving. "It's brutal," says Matt. He loves to take pictures of bugs stuck in Venus Flytraps. He tells me that whenever he finds a praying mantis, the great creature turns to look at him, virtually making eye contact. He loves it. Maybe we are all hunters.

And maybe in our hunting, we really end up gathering. One day in 2008, my dad called to say that some of his plants would be featured in the season premiere of *CSI: New York*. A producer in search of "sensitive plants" (strange little plants that fold their leaves when touched) had found plenty at *www.hirts.com*, had bought the entire inventory, and had paid to have them shipped overnight to the studio. The huge sale stoked my dad and brother with excitement. According to Dad, the plants would be featured in the cliffhanging last scene, when the mystery killer lowers his hands over the plants and they fold their leaves as if in prayer. Sinister prayer, of course.

I couldn't wait to watch the episode, to know that of the millions of viewers, only a few of us knew where those plants came from. I looked forward to gathering that story, to making it one more pane of glass in the only greenhouse I could rebuild.

Near a Fine Woods
Finishing my Grandmother's Journal

When my grandparents moved into assisted living in 2002, my dad searched their attic for Grandpa's rumored stash of money, but instead he found Grandma's journal. He called me in Idaho, where I was in graduate school, and wondered if I might like to have the journal on my next visit to Ohio. I started making travel plans that day.

My grandparents, Hobart and Onalee Hirt, were hardworking Midwesterners who didn't waste time with their full names. Hobart went by Hob, rhyming with the biblical Job, and Onalee went by Ony, pronounced as "Ah-ni." In 1943, they purchased twenty-three acres a quarter mile away from the greenhouses. Grandpa's brother secured a neighboring parcel. They each built modest homes and raised families, textbook chapters in the great America dream.

My grandmother's journal was one of those chapters, and I needed it more than usual because I'd grown cynical about my family. Come summer break, I couldn't cross time zones fast enough.

The first thing I noticed about the journal was that Ony had given it a title, "The Woods." I flipped the yellowed pages of the hardbound accounting ledger; thirty-five pages of entries, covering half a century, followed by two hundred and seventy blank pages. She had scripted a brief introduction, and in its tone and details I could tell that my grandmother had written this for a later reader as well as for herself.

Way back in 1938 Hob pointed out this spot to me as the perfect location for our home. I readily agreed for it was beautiful. There was a hill by a small creek, very near a fine woods, one quarter mile from the center and the greenhouse, on a paved road.

They could hardly wait to build a house. But what was the first thing they did, as soon as the deed was signed? On November 18, 1943, they planted twenty-five hickory trees and twenty-five willows.

The winter must have been mild (and a new house not so urgent), for the next months document a planting spree of unrivaled magnitude. "Dressed for the woods Hob and I set out to plant our long planned orchard." A grove of four apples, four peaches, three plums, three cherries, two pears, one quince. An elm. Twenty-four walnuts. Five oaks along the wagon road, which would soon extend into a driveway lined with oaks. Below the young forest, they nestled clusters of buttercups, ivy, and myrtle.

Reading Ony's proud narrative, I realized I had never planted a tree, nor dreamt of a starting an orchard. I tabulated the various tree planting notes over the next six months—one hundred and eighty trees. As I child, I'd walked through the woods (sometimes with Grandma, sometimes with cousins, sometimes with parents), and no one ever mentioned the old orchard. What had become of it? The journal gave no clues.

Next, her journal documented how Christmas came and went that year, and there were still no architecture plans, but a mid-January blizzard inspired a tobogganing party complete with "a fire to keep us warm, with the help of something for snakebite." Something for snakebite. I turned the phrase in my mind. Did she mean frostbite? Then *something* decoded itself as *liquor*. I pictured flasks of whisky and rum. It sounded

My grandparents in 1939

like the most fun ever. To hell with building a house! They were young. They ran their own business. Their corner of the world held nothing but potential. I wished I could have known their snow.

The honeymoon with the woods lasted two solid years, and not a single discouraging entry appears. Then, two years to the day after the genesis of the orchard, there is this ever-so-subtle awareness. Something was changing. Fourteen months had passed between entries. Time, as always, was escaping.

November 18, 1945
After a period of being much too busy at things that just had to be, we found time to wander down to "the woods." I would have liked to plant

some narcissi among it this fall but there doesn't seem to be any bulbs—so that can wait along with the building of our house. But much to Hob's satisfaction the Chinese Chestnuts did take hold.

I wondered if Ony was weary of the rigorous horticultural life, was wanting the pretty horticultural life. Not the heavy saplings and labor-intensive holes they needed and then the long wait for maturity; instead, delicate bulbs and pretty wildflowers. I read her comment about the exotic Chinese Chestnuts and juxtapose it with the longing for the tender yellow narcissus, a flower *she* wanted, a flower guaranteed to be hardy and self-sufficient, *something just for her,* or maybe a house, *how about a house, Hob.* I realized patience was being tested.

In January 1947, Hob had paid fifty dollars to a local architect, C.W. Richards, and the house was finally being planned. Ony and Hob chose a hilltop area for the homestead. The valley slanted to the east and south, like a crescent, and the woods extended everywhere from the hilltop. Ony spearheaded an effort to clear underbrush.

Our building plot looks promising after a few good fires. Something has really spurred us on in the idea of building, so much so that we have dared to see a builder and start our plans (maybe it was these fires, not that we have enough money, but we do have nerve).

Nineteen months pass before the next entry, in August 1948. There are financial problems. "We were planning to build to the tune of thirty thousand dollars and didn't know it." There is not enough money, and not even Ony's self-deprecating tone can ease the matter. The home they want, with a garage, three bedrooms, two baths, a laundry room, and a dining room, is too extravagant. The journal falls silent until May 22, 1949, when a simple sentence resurrects all hope. "We're at it again." Perhaps the spring sales at the greenhouse exceeded their highest expectations.

From here, there are almost daily updates through June 1949. The basement was dug, bedrock blasted, water lines laid, septic tank and filter readied for service. In July, "the basement, now covered, is most beautiful." By the first of August, Ony wrote, "Now we know what it will look like. It is wonderful." They worked into autumn, siding, plas-

My grandmother and me in the greenhouse, circa 1976

tering, painting. By mid-December, the home was almost finished. "The fireplace is perfect, everything is perfect."

Hob and Ony and their three children (my father, a toddler, was the youngest), moved in on Christmas Eve, 1949. My grandmother must have been exhausted. She wrote just one line to commemorate. "All set for the best Christmas ever, and a week off to enjoy it."

It's tough for me to picture my dad growing up in the house. I can only recall the Christmas morning photo of the three children tumbling down the new stairs. My grandparents never hung family photos on the wall, and I never saw a family portrait. It makes me realize that in the journal, Ony did not record the births of her children. There are only entries about the woods and the house.

After the jubilant Christmas, Ony only wrote in her journal three times over four decades. A 1951 entry reaffirms how wonderful the house has become.

We are well settled, as if we had been here for years. We have a beautiful lawn. The woods and the valley are a lovely lacy green. Soon there will be many blossoms on the crabs and dogwoods. Our drive is a picture with bluette and daffodils. The birds are innumerable. The woods is the best place in the world for "cowboys and Indians." Marie, Clare, and Alan hit the trail every chance they get; they never tire of it. They have beaten paths in every direction.

And it is here, with all dreams realized, with all futures secured, that the journal lies dormant not for months, not even for a clutch of years, but for decades.

What history can I contribute to the silence? In the fifties, Grandpa splurged on a rare luxury, an inground swimming pool, and it was an instant neighborhood favorite. By the seventies, when the children were grown, married, and running the business, Grandpa built himself a huge greenhouse around the pool. He became obsessed with African violets, tending to them in the humidity created by the pool. Me, my brother, and our cousins spent entire weekends swimming and having contests—like who could splash water to the highest panes of glass? Grandpa would fuss over his violets, and Grandma would shell peas, and all around us, outside, was the deep green of the woods.

As the grandkids grew up and lost interest in the pool, other changes happened, too. By the nineties, the Hirt's land was one of the last bastions in a city sprawling with subdivisions and commerce. Developers had already built a colossal mall just down the road from the woods, and there was more to come.

By 1993, the year I graduated high school, real estate agents practically camped at my grandparents' doorstep. They offered millions, and my grandparents accepted. They sold the woods to Wald & Fisher, Inc.

While Ony had not written in her journal since 1951, she went back to it in 1994, in an entry dated only with the year. She picked up right where she left off forty-three years ago.

After many years of enjoying our home, valley, creek and woods, the cowboys and Indians have grown up...all three are married and have their own homes. Also we have four grandchildren and one great-grandchild. Our home has meant much to all of us; but times have changed.

Strongsville has changed; it has become a city; much traffic with the coming of the Ohio Turnpike and Interstate 71 and many allotments and businesses. Our woods, valley, creek, and home are right in the middle of it. With a large office building on one side and a shopping center planned on the other, it will never be the same.

And the final entry, from January 15, 1994:

We have sold our woods and home. We have a "life estate," hoping the remembrances will make it possible for us to stay here many years.

The "life estate" meant that my grandparents would receive the money from the sale immediately but could continue to live in the house. When they moved out or died, Wald & Fisher, Inc. would take immediate ownership.

I wish, in 1994, when I was absorbed in my first year of college, that I had spoken up about the sale. I wish I had been a little wiser, more confident, less apathetic, able to present alternatives. Why not obtain a conservation easement, or donate it to the city as a park? I wish I had known about the journal, and also had the insight that lets me read it the way I read it now. I wish I had known that when you return to a journal after forty-three years, you do it for a powerful reason.

Not long after the contracts were filed and money was exchanged, Wald & Fisher bulldozed the forest on the seventeen acres around my grandparents' house and greenhouse. They chainsawed the oaks lining the driveway, saplings planted half a century before, the splendid oaks forever in my rearview memory as I'm squirming in the backseat of my mom's car after a day of swimming in the pool in the greenhouse. Thousands of parking spaces flattened the natural contours. The big box retailers laid their grids. Wald & Fisher filled in part of the valley to build a wide entrance. They filled it in, turfed it, erected a sign: *Welcome to The Greens of Strongsville.*

Away at college, I heard bits of news from my parents. They said my grandparents were shocked. They had not expected such swiftness, such total revamping of land that they had known for a lifetime. I wondered whether my grandparents were manipulated or just ignorant of modern development.

My grandparents' private greenhouse, summer 2002

At first, they tried to make the best of it. Grandma liked having the grocery so close. But the new store was too big, too confusing, and she stumbled on the cobblestone floor of the produce section. She and Grandpa tried the TGIFriday's one night, but the "neighborhood grill" atmosphere was loud and distracting. They couldn't hear their server, the portions were too large and too expensive, and the lighting was dim. They couldn't understand why the place was packed every night. With the towering oaks and pines gone, the lights from the parking lot shone into their bedroom. They stopped sitting outside in the evenings. Fearful of strangers, Grandpa erected a chain link fence with an automatic locking gate. They stopped gardening.

Finally, they took to worrying about the money from the sale. How much were they supposed to receive? Had they received it? Confusion grew like weeds in their minds. For so many years my grandparents had

*The fire department using my grandparents' house for
a controlled practice burn, September 29, 2002*

been business partners, able to scrape by in hard times and hand a
business to their sons. Now, with most of their land "developed" into
a shopping destination, it was as if their concept of finances had been
bulldozed and discarded. While the "life estate" gave them the money
they wanted, it obliterated their sense of true security. Their health
started to fail that year, dementia for Hob, osteoporosis for Ony, and
heart problems for both. In 2002, they went into assisted living. Two
weeks into the new arrangement, my grandpa died of a heart attack. It
was the only two weeks he'd spent away from home. Grandma would
die within the year.

When I read my grandmother's journal on a summer day in 2002,
I did one other thing. I walked through every room of the house, and
tried to remember it all, because Wald & Fisher were days away from

*What was built where my grandparents' house and
private greenhouse used to be, winter 2003*

owning it. I took books from the built-in shelves near the fireplace,
including an early edition of *Walden* and all of Ony's Greek and Latin
textbooks, with her studious notes in the margins from her college days
at Baldwin-Wallace, and a little-used family Bible, dated 1895. I slid
my hands through her wardrobe; bedridden, she did not need these
clothes. I selected a sleeveless denim work dress with pockets, her practical style. I took a painting of roses. An inscription on the back was
from the cousin who had painted it. *A little late! But happy 50th wedding
anniversary!* In the attic I found an exquisite Japanese teacup with a dragon
molded in raised china around its circumference, and I tucked it in the
pocket of the denim dress.

Next, I went to the old greenhouse and pool. The pool had long been
drained and covered with wooden slats. Some tropical palms Grandpa had
been tending were now dead, too. But all around the outside of the greenhouse, the verdant summer throb of wild plants pressed against the glass.

Ivy, vines, branches, grass. The foliage pressed up the sides of the green-house, had sprouted through cracks, had tangled itself in corners and around pipes. Every leaf wanted in, and why not? Greenhouses are never supposed to be empty. Standing there in that emptiness, I thought about the 270 empty pages in Ony's journal. Maybe she had left them for me.

September 29, 2002

Ony, I am thankful that you do not know what has happened to your home. Wald & Fisher let the Strongsville Fire Department use it as a practice fire. I guess it was a fast and free way to clear the land.

Dad called me in Idaho as your house burned. He was taking photos that he would eventually hang in his office. I had nothing to say. I said I was sorry. He said, *"There goes the roof."* I asked how close he was. He said behind the police tape. I was silent. I was trying to hear the fire over the phone lines. I couldn't. I hated everyone in the parking lot, every-one gawking at the fire as they passed by on their way to shopping at the Greens of Strongsville. I would have screamed at them.

December 27, 2002

There isn't much to see. Heavy wet snow covers the barren expanse. Some industrial-looking pipes stick out, probably groundwork for future plumbing. I'm sitting in my car. I've driven all the way from Idaho. Either I feel nothing or I feel a huge blankness. I can't get angry or wistful. It is like the space is dead.

December 27, 2003

Ony, they've built a Famous Footwear over the foundation of your house and a Pier 1 over the foundation of your greenhouse. There are probably one thousand parking spaces where I think the grove must have been. In strips of soil in concrete medians, there are eighty spindly trees, all the same. It is just like every other shopping center.

December 28, 2007

I'm here again, trying to remember again. I walk behind the shop-ping center and stare into the valley. Orange carts, plastic bags, bottles.

The usual. Even the leaves look like trash. I can see the dark creek but I can't hear it over the traffic. I follow deer tracks along the guardrail until I convince myself I'm oriented with the faint trailhead, that starting point of tobogganing and long walks. I turn and face the service entry of Pier I, trying to remember the greenhouse and the pool. Nothing comes back. The emptiness in my memory is maddening. I need something for snakebite.

I head into Pier I. Inside, I stand for a minute, pulling off my hat and mittens and getting my bearings among the imported chintz of wine glasses and wicker. Then I see it. Along the wall is a display of Greenhouse and Grove Candles. I walk straight to them. I am dreaming. I am dying. I am so disconnected and so profoundly connected that I think I have to stop breathing to make this moment last forever, to make it fill 270 pages.

The greenhouse candles are called Crisp Bamboo, Tuscan Herb, and Citrus Cilantro. The grove candles are Mango Papaya, Ginger Peach, and, strangely, Ember. There are three sizes, from pillars to votives. The scents come in oils and spray bottles too. Everything is made in Vietnam.

Ony, I have recently read that nature should not be thought of as what we see but how we see. When nature is "what" we see, we are the consumer, and nature is a scented candle wrapped in plastic. I am sure, seventy years ago, that you knew this.

For the first time, I feel like I understand your journal. The nature that isn't here is showing me how to see. I'm leaving Pier I and I'm not buying anything. I'm sure I never have to come back. Like you wrote in your journal, I too see a very fine woods. Those woods are no longer here, but they are not too far away.

Sources

Many of my essays involved research beyond the standard family discussion. I am grateful to all these articles, books, and websites for the facts that lead to insight. I have grouped the bibliographic entries according to essay and have included explanatory notes when necessary. I should note that I have included a couple of personal interviews, but I cannot attach clear dates to all the conversations I've had with my family, given the ongoing nature of informal family discussions.

Glass Always Breaks

Hix, John. *The Glass House*. London: Phaidon Press Limited, 1996.
    The tattoo comes from an image on page 8, a 1783 blueprint designed by Pieter de la Court van de Voort. The four trees depicted at the beginning of each essay also come from this image. The tattoo was done by Brooks Jenkins of Little City Tattoos in Moscow, Idaho.

Under Glass

Other than informal discussions with my father and the reference to an email message, the only other source I used was two poorly photocopied pages from what appears to be a "History of Strongsville" publication, something that served as a commemorative booklet, I think. My mom gave me the photocopy and wrote "article from 1968 magazine" at the bottom. The entry is titled "Hirt's Greenhouse," and is credited to Maude Roy Hirt, my grandpa's sister-in-law. I used this article for verification of dates, and it also appears on the epigraph page.

Controlling the Light

Hix, John. *The Glass House*. London: Phaidon Press Limited, 1996.

Woods, May and Arete Swartz Warren. *Glasshouses: A History of Greenhouses, Orangeries, and Conservatories*. New York: Rizzoli, 1988.

When the Disease Process Cannot be Compared to Volcanic Island Chains

Hegi, Ursula. *Tearing the Silence*. New York: Simon and Schuster, 1997.
    Although I did not mention this book specifically, Hegi's insights into silence gave me a starting point for approaching silence in my family.

Hirt, Karen. Personal interview. 29 December 2003.

Joy, Janet E. and Richard B. Johnston, Jr., eds. *Multiple Sclerosis: Current Status and Strategies for the Future*. Washington, D.C.: National Academy Press, 2001.
    This source provided background info on MS.

Poser, Charles M. *An Atlas of Multiple Sclerosis*. New York: The Parthenon Publishers Group, 1998.

Sontag, Susan. *Illness as Metaphor and AIDS and its Metaphors*. Anchor Books edition. New York: Doubleday Anchor Books, 1990.

Into the Teeth of It

Bowers, Neal. *Theodore Roethke: The Journey from I to Otherwise*. Columbia: University of Missouri Press, 1982.
    This source provided background information on Roethke.

Malkoff, Karl. *Theodore Roethke: An Introduction to the Poetry.* New York: Columbia University Press, 1966.

The Roethke family greenhouses are described in Chapter One, titled "The Greenhouse Land." Chapter Three, "News of the Root," is an analysis of the greenhouse poems. This analysis helped me understand Roethke's themes.

R.E.M. *Automatic for the People.* Warner Bros., 1992.

The phrase "automatic for the people" is a reference to this recording.

Roethke, Theodore. "An American Poet Introduces Himself and His Poems." BBC broadcast. July 30, 1953. Rpt. In *On Poetry and Craft.* By Theodore Roethke. Port Townsend, Washington: Copper Canyon Press, 2001.

From this source comes the quote, "They were to me, I realize now, both heaven and hell, a kind of tropics created in the savage climate of Michigan, where austere German Americans turned their love of order and their terrifying efficiency into something truly beautiful . . . ."

———. *Straw for the Fire.* Seattle: University of Washington Press, 1980.

This is an edited collection of Roethke's journals.

———. *The Collected Poems of Theodore Roethke.* Anchor Books edition. New York: Doubleday Anchor Books, 1975.

The title for this essay comes from Roethke's poem "Big Wind."

Wolff, George. *Theodore Roethke.* Boston: Twayne Publishers, 1981.

This source provided some history behind the greenhouse poems.

Cut

Harvey, Matthea. *Pity the Bathtub its Forced Embrace of the Human Form.* Farmington: Alice James Books, 2000.

Healy, Dermot. *The Bend Toward Home.* New York: Harcourt Brace, 1998.

Hirt, Ed. Personal scrapbook. Circa 1945.

Pynchon, Thomas. *Gravity's Rainbow.* New York: Penguin, 1973.

R.E.M. "Country Feedback." *Out of Time.* Warner Bros., 1991.

Roethke, Theodore. *The Collected Poems of Theodore Roethke.* Anchor Books edition. New York: Doubleday Anchor Books, 1975.

The Grotto of the Redemption

"Grotto of the Redemption." Homepage. http://www.westbendgrotto. com. Accessed multiple times during spring 2002.

Ricinus Communis

Barber, Mike. "Spokane Man Held on Poison Charge." *Seattle Post-Intelligencer.* June 20, 2002.

I used this article (and others like it) to doublecheck my facts and to confirm the timeline of the Olsen case.

Barnaby, Wendy, *The Plague Makers.* New York: Continuum, 2000.

This source provided great details about previous ricin cases.

Blocker, Kevin. "Olsen's ex-lover defends him." *Spokesman Review.* July 8, 2003. B3.

Crone, Hugh. *Banning Chemical Weapons.* Cambridge University Press, 1992.

Here I found the narratives of ricin assassinations (and attempted assassinations).

Douglass, Joseph D. and Neil C. Livingstone. *America the Vulnerable.* Massachusetts: Lexington Books, 1987.

This source gave information about the CIA double agent.

Durant, Mary. *Who Named the Daisy? Who Named the Rose?* New York: Dodd, Mead, and Company, 1976.

This source provided the origin of how the castor bean got its name.

Endicott, Stephen and Edward Hagerman. *The United States and Biological Warfare.* Bloomington, Indiana University Press, 1998.

The source provided the history of the BWC set-up in 1944, as well as Proctor and Gamble's involvement in developing ricin.

Geissler, Erhard, and John Ellis van Courtland Moon, editors. *Biological and Toxin Weapons: Research, Development and Use from the Middle Ages to 1945.* Oxford: Oxford University Press, 1999.

I read about Horn Island in this source.

Harden, Blaine. "Ingredients for unusual trial: A triangle and toxic ricin." *The Washington Post.* April 5, 2003. A3.

———. "Judge won't dismiss ricin case." *Spokesman Review.* November 9, 2002. B3.

Harris, Robert and Jeremy Paxman. *A Higher Form of Killing.* New York:
    Hill and Wang, 1982.
    This source provided the clearest narrative regarding the Bulgarian
    dissidents targeted with ricin.
Martin, Jonathan. "Family rallies around poison suspect." *Spokesman
    Review.* June 21, 2002. A1.
Morlin, Bill. "Suspect remains in jail." *Spokesman Review.* July 2, 2002.
    B1.
———. "Ricin case reads like pulp fiction." *Spokesman Review.* January 12,
    2003. B1.
———. "Ricin defense gets trial delay." *Spokesman Review.* January 22,
    2003. B1.
———. "Judge refuses to release ricin suspect." *Spokesman Review.* Febru-
    ary 11, 2003. B1.
———. "Arkansas man testifies he sold poison." *Spokesman Review.* March
    6, 2003. B1.
———. "No gag order for ricin suspect's wife." *Spokesman Review.* July 1,
    2003. B1.
———. "Olsen's motive benign, lawyer says." *Spokesman Review.* July 2,
    2003. B1.
———. "Scientist says Olsen intended to make ricin." *Spokesman Review.*
    July 15, 2003. B2.
———. "Defense witness questions testing process." *Spokesman Review.* July
    16, 2003. B2.
———. "Man facing ricin charges stays off stand." *Spokesman Review.* July
    17, 2003. B2.
———. "Man guilty in ricin case." *Spokesman Review.* July 18, 2003. A1.
———. "Ricin maker sentenced." *Spokesman Review.* October 29, 2003.
    B5.
Moshkin, V.A., editor. *Castor.* Translated under agreement with the US
    Department of Agriculture, translated by R.K. Dhote. Kolos publishers,
    Moscow, 1980. translated edition. New Dehli: Oxonian Press, 1986.
Nappi, Rebecca. "Friends wait with you, even in times of trial." Com-
    mentary. *Spokesman Review.* July 19, 2003.

Rodkey, Chris. "Wife supports husband as ricin case looms." *Associated Press*. June 28, 2003.

Turner, Nancy and Adam Szczawinski. *Common Poisonous Plants and Mushrooms of North America*. Portland: Timber Press, 1991.

This source helped me understand how ricin poisons cells.

Wiley, John K. "Jury convicts software engineer of making ricin." *Moscow-Pullman Daily News*. July 18, 2003. A3.

Stronghold

Keller, Helen. *The Story of My Life*. New York: Doubleday, 1954.

Radiohead. "Everything in its right place." *Kid A*. EMI Records, 2000.

Roethke, Theodore. *Straw for the Fire*. Seattle: University of Washington Press, 1980.

The sentence "Every pretty thing in its right place" is a blended allusion to a song by Radiohead and an entry in one of Roethke's journals.

Laying Dynamite with the Ninth Duke of Devonshire

Colquhon, Kate. *A Thing in Disguise: The Visionary Life of Joseph Paxton*. London: Fourth Estate, 2003.

Colquhon's biography of Paxton is fantastic – I gleaned many details from her astute research on Paxton. Many of the facts about Paxton I already knew from other sources listed below.

Elliot, Charles. "Water lily fit for a queen." *Horticulture*. Jan. 1996, vol. 74.1. 20-24.

Emboden, William A. *Bizarre Plants: Magical, Monstrous, Mythical*. New York: Macmillan, 1974.

My sentence, "Would Paxton have added that natives of the Canary Islands, where Europeans had first seen the dragon tree a century prior, believed that since the venerable trees bled, they also had souls?" is a paraphrase of material from this source.

Harold and Maude. Dir. Hal Ashby. Perf. Ruth Gordon, Bud Cort. Paramount, 1971.

Hix, John. *The Glass House*. London: Phaidon Press Limited, 1996.
Chapter 6, "The Private Conservatory," provided factual details
about Joseph Paxton, the Dukes of Devonshire, and the Great
Conservatory. This chapter has stunning juxtaposed photos of the
Great Conservatory in its prime and then in 1920. I used these
photos in my imaginative recreations of the Great Conservatory.
This source also provided the quote on the epigraph page attrib-
uted to Paul Scheerbart.

Lehner, Ernst and Johanna. *Folklore and Symbolism of Flowers, Plants, and
Trees*. New York: Tudor Publishing, 1960.
The lore of the dragon tree comes from this source. Artwork about
the dragon tree figured into my descriptions. The entire section
about Yggdrasill comes from this source.

"The Conservatory Garden and Maze." Homepage. http://www.chats-
worth-house.co.uk Accessed November 5, 2003.

Woods, May and Arete Swartz Warren. *Glasshouses: A History of Greenhouses, Orangeries, and Conservatories*. New York: Rizzoli, 1988.
Chapter 5, "The Victorian Glasshouse," provided factual details
about Joseph Paxton, the Dukes of Devonshire, and the Great
Conservatory. It also provided the list of plants in the Great Conservatory.

Near a Fine Woods

Heileman, David. "Shopping center plans to expand." *The Strongsville
Sun*. August 22, 2002. Online. www.sunnews.com. Accessed Novem-
ber 4, 2002.
Information about Wald & Fisher comes from this source.

Hirt, Onalee. Personal journal, 1943–1994.